Great Men Think ~~Alike~~ - Like God

You Have the Mind of Christ

Tarshish Productions
Elkhart, Indiana

Linda C. Newberry

Published by Tarshish Productions, 1933 N Stone Maple Lane, Elkhart, Indiana 46514.

Unless otherwise noted, Scripture quotations are taken from the King James Bible.

References to Strong's are taken from the Strong's Exhaustive Concordance in both book and electronic form.

Dictionary definitions mentioned are from Webster's, MacMillan and WordNet online Dictionaries

ISBN-10: 0976964066
ISBN-13: 978-0-9769640-6-3

www.lindacnewberry.com
Printed in the United States of America

Table of Contents

Acknowledgements

Thank you to Benjamin Franklin, Thomas Edison, Albert Einstein and Napoleon Hill. These men were thinkers who underwent adversity, delays and yes, even defeat in the process of turning the thoughts in their mind into the products, institutions and theories that have shaped our world.

Aided by help from above, they were able to achieve more than most men. They did it through believing they "were onto something" and perseverance to see it through.

Their tenacity has influenced me and will continue to do so.

Introduction

Yesterday I posted this on Facebook:

We talk a lot here about our thinking....what we choose to think, catching ourselves thinking things that serve no useful purpose to our direction or our goals, and deciding that when we find useless thoughts invading our mind....we stop and re-think with useful thoughts. This is similar to re-tooling a failing piece of machinery. You take out the failing tool and replace it with a new and functional tool to allow you to produce the desired end result. This is our life and thinking our tool to be useful and productive. ~ Linda C Newberry *FB post 7/14/2013*

I have often wondered at the seeming gap between what God has placed in our heart and what we see in the material world around us. Proverb 13:12 that tells us "Hope deferred makes the heart sick…" I have been pondering this verse and many others lately.

If we get engrossed in this part of the verse, it can begin to breed unrest. We begin to wonder why that vision hasn't developed yet, is it a wrong vision, did we do something to short-stop it, was I wrong, or was it just a pipe dream? However if we look at the balance of the verse "…but *when* the desire comes, it is a tree of life," we can then again begin to feel strength pour into our life.

It is wrong thinking that gets us into trouble before we know God and wrong thinking that creates (or maintains) obstacles after we know Him. I understand that the use of the word “wrong” could be considered controversial in the world which we live, but stop and think about it.

Uninformed thinking is wrong thinking. Skewed vision of a circumstance is wrong thinking. Taking information fed to us by government or media can, in many instances, be wrong thinking (more often than not, as this has been proven through the ages). Succumbing to negative tapes that play in our heads and acting according to what we hear rather than believing what God has said about us is wrong thinking.

Wrong thinking comes when we take up even slight variations on the truth found in His word. His word is our standard of good living, but it is not the only thing. We need to make sure that we are being receptive to the wisdom and knowledge he leads us to during different phases of our lives.

Without first understanding the truth of His word, the vast volumes of detail about most any subject we would like to study, and about the manipulation perpetrated against the masses in our banking systems, education, government, social class and day-to-day business, we can and often do become a puppet on a string rather than the person in charge.

It is up to us to seek truth and then choose whether to engage fully or remain on the sidelines, no matter which we choose, it starts in our thinking.

Good morning, Father. Bible study can come in many forms. As I begin to re-read the text of your word, I am also branching out into some educational reading that has come my way, no doubt, by your hand. I pray for these who join me and are nudged to do some reading of things that will make them think and expand their vision for their lives. We praise you for favor that wraps us up and goes before us in all we do. Help us to move past fear, or anger, or contentment to remain at status quo. Give us the desire to move past our original thought of who we are today and expand into the person/life/influence that one step past our former understanding has created. Give us the courage to be all that you designed us to be, and show us today those we are to be of greatest service to. In Jesus' name, we praise and thank you, Amen!

CHAPTER 1

How do I Study? What Path Do I Take?

Good morning all! Just wanted to take a minute or two to give you a preemptive statement about this new line of study. You will get a bird's eye view of how I go about studying and the process I use over the course of this study.

Up to this point the subject matter of our emails and blog posts has been verses, or a series of verses that I've studied at some period in the past. I had an idea of the underlying message within these verses, because I'd used most of them to confess and/or affirm my faith. But in this study, the impression for me to understand more about the thinking process and its importance for us to live our lives more fully, not just personally, but, generationally has been strong.

At some point I have no doubt read the verses that we will be studying, or studied out the individual verse for its blessing potential. I have not done it based from the idea of our thought mechanism though. Hopefully you will stick with this, as I believe there is something here for all of us, but I am not sure what gems we will pull out of these studies.

To begin with, I pulled up a list of scriptures that had anything to do with renewing the mind. Then rather than getting all of the definitions within the verse, I only got the

Strong's Concordance definition of the words that would pertain to the mind or thought or its process.

Yesterday we began the study with a verse that was in the middle of the list. My original thought for today's study was to leave it at that and move to the next verse on the list, but then I looked up the number of times that this word translated "affection" was used. 37 times in 21 verses.

I want to know what God has to say about this word meaning "to exercise the mind." Where does He apply this word and its meaning? What does this mean we have to look for and does it affect our every action? I believe in this study we will see the answers to these questions (and probably others) emerge.

So beginning tomorrow we will delve into this set of verses and see what we uncover. You may see that rather than studying out each of these verses we will group some together based on a similar message or we may go one by one, until I get into this I will not know. For now let's look at the God balance we might want to see in our lives.

I recently heard a teaching cautioning against too much thought. If not explained more fully there will be some who don't have a balanced walk who could begin to feel that they are to set everything aside to seek only what they perceive as the things of God.

Some may have this kind of time, but others also have family and work that eat up a great deal of time. So how do we maneuver into "God balance." True balance in the kingdom is not like a scale with separate "life segment" containers hanging from a fulcrum point called "Our Life."

This scale would look like this: "Our Life" as the fulcrum and the buckets divided up as follows: God with all things spiritual; Family with wife, children, parents, siblings, etc.; Work or entrepreneurial pursuits and finances; Health, both physical and emotional, mental pursuits; Social with friends and fun; Community with involvement in the local, state, country and world.

This paints a picture of us being the center of our world, the fulcrum (the point on which an object turns or balances; the person or thing that everything else depends on). God is a section of this picture of life rather than the blanket that covers and the scent that permeates the life. "God" is not only a Sunday thing or that thing we seek when everything else is out of balance. So we hop from the "Community" bucket over to God when things are out of balance, or from the "Financial" or "Health" bucket to the "God" bucket to see what he can add to bring balance.

But our balance as children of God has a different look to it. God is that point on which our life depends; it is the point on which our life turns and is balanced. This picture has two fulcrum points, and our scale needs to looks more like this.

"God/the spiritual" is our first fulcrum point, he is the creator of "Our Life" and is invested, fully invested in our success. The word invested means officially endowed fully with authority or power over. This means that He has power and authority over our life and all the buckets under that. However, He also invests into "Our Life." The word invest means to provide <u>us</u> with power and authority, being placed formally in an office or position (as ambassadors in the earth) and to give qualities and abilities to (that help us to generate our work, income and help for others), these are tools we use to create "Our Life."

When we use these tools, we advance. In order to use these tools, we are required to exercise our minds. The word ability means possession of the qualities (especially mental qualities) required to do something or get something done. We learn about them and how to use them to our advantage.

"Our Life" becomes in this picture the second fulcrum, not the first, and the baskets would be named; Family/wife, children, parents, siblings, etc.; Work/entrepreneurial pursuits and finances; Health/physical, emotional, mental pursuits; Social/friends and fun; Community/involvement in the local, state, country and world.

To have a properly functioning and balanced "Our Life," we need to take the tools (the position, abilities, power and authority) He provided us with and exercise them in our life. This means we need to exercise this mind/thought/brain muscle as filtered through God's principles. As we do this in these separate buckets of our lives (always understanding that God is not a bucket, but a pivot point) a godly balance is created.

There is a part of the teacher's line of thought that I do agree with. Too often we are asked "what do you think" or we offer up opinions on matters that we know little to nothing about. The crux of the verse Colossians 3:2 from yesterday is "we exercise our mind on things above, not on the things of the earth". But rather than think that the only thinking we have to do is to continue to think of heaven, let's look at this from the vantage point that we are to filter all information brought to us through a filter to God's way of thinking and doing.

You see; He did not give us this glorious brain to lie dormant and only seek him. He already has a heaven full of angels that honor and glorify Him day in and out. Our way of glorifying Him includes the things we do and get done for humanity here in this earth. And in order to be effective at whatever our piece of the puzzle is, we need to use this brain/mind/thought process machine along with inspiration from him that enters through this mechanism to its greatest advantage.

Good morning, Father. Thank you so much for guiding us through this study. I am not sure where this will take us, but am grateful for the opportunity to look at this. We have seen examples of people throughout history who have made a great impact on society and helped people through the thinking process. You have called us sheep in your Word, with you as our shepherd, we are asking for help to understand that we are your sheep and not the sheep of every person or organization or politician that clamors for us to follow them blindly. You gave us a mind and heart to discern. Part of our discernment comes from your truth, and part of it comes from revealed facts. We are to seek you first, and this one statement leads us to understand that there are other things you sent us here to do. Show us the next step to take and we praise and thank you in Jesus' name for favor in our endeavors, Amen!

Definitions used in today's study:
Affection - from <G5424> (phren); to exercise the mind, i.e. entertain or have a sentiment or opinion; by implication to be

(mentally) disposed (more or less earnestly in a certain direction); intensive to interest oneself in (with concern or obedience) :- set the affection on, (be) care (-ful), (be like-, + be of one, + be of the same, + let this) mind (-ed), regard, savour, think; probably from an obsolete phrao (to rein in or curb; compare <G5420> (phrasso)); the midrif (as a partition of the body), i.e. (figurative and by implication of sympathy) the feelings (or sensitive nature; by extension [also in the plural] the mind or cognitive faculties) :- understanding.

CHAPTER 2

Exercise the Mind

Colossians 3:2 (KJV)

2 Set your affection (exercise the mind, entertain or have sentiment or opinion, be mentally disposed or make receptive or involve the mind or intellectual process/willing towards an action or attitude or belief) on things above, not on things on the earth.

Monday I mentioned a line of understanding that I have been pursuing, thinking. Thinking happens when we seek new knowledge, when we read a book (any book), when we watch a show on television, when we talk to a friend, when we sit at our desk at work, when we drive down the road and when we close our eyes lying in bed at the end of the day.

Thinking occurs in the mind. In a wide sense it means to use or exercise the mind or one's power of reason in order to make inferences, decisions, or arrive at a solution or judgments. To keep it narrow it means to have something in your mind.

As Wikipedia puts it "A mind is the set of cognitive faculties that enables consciousness, perception, thinking, judgment, and memory—a characteristic of humans." We have something in this mind from the time we open our eyes in the morning until we drift off at night, and truth be known our mind is still active in the silent hours during our sleeping hours.

Proper use and control of the thoughts in our mind is key to every area of our life. A problem that I have experienced in my life and see in so many others out there is that it is just so easy to float through life, in essence, allowing others to do our research and thinking for us.

We have given up responsibility of solid decision making to people who could care less about our lives and only want to manipulate us with their version of the facts or truth. We then make decisions based on corrupt information.

Sometimes the information is corrupt in the idea of being dishonest, illegal, or immoral, with some personalized ulterior motive behind it. Sometimes it is corrupt in the idea of it having been originated in truth but through multiplied telling and "as I remember it" from person to person the truth of the matter is near unrecognizable by the time it gets to us.

When I use the word corrupt here it is not necessarily to imply meanness of spirit, but instead to say we need to see most information coming to us as suspicious. Even the Bible teaching we hear, needs to be investigated by us.

The Holy Spirit acts as an internal radar to falsehood. Some people who are not aware of his presence in our lives may call it intuition or a sixth sense.

We are to exercise our minds, using our intellectual gifts as well as our ability to hear the Holy Spirit speak to us.

When we hear something from a Bible teacher or pastor it is our responsibility to not take it at face value and study it out on our own.

The Bible contains the original truth to base our thought life, our speech and our actions on. The faith we have is the faith of God, and the hope (or expectation) that this faith will work is cultivated not only by prayer but by the use of this magnificent thinking process that goes on second by second in our mind.

The mind cannot be separated from our faith. Instead, I will say that it is an integral part of the hope/faith building process. Instead of manipulation by other people or a belief system (whether spiritual, financial, political or social), isn't it time for us to take responsibility for and begin to manipulate (to skillfully handle, control, or use something) our own thinking? Is it not better that as this word says, to exercise our mind by processing the information that is brought to us?

We have lost control of an inordinate amount of our liberties due to floating through life, sleeping and allowing others to wiggle and maneuver. Rather than floating through life it is important to wake up, be led by the spirit to truths in the Bible and other texts that will help us change our world and not only maintain our remaining freedoms, but regain those which have been temporarily lost.

Good morning, Father. Thank you for leading us in this study. Give us the willingness to take responsibility for our thoughts…you have given us the means to change our internal and external landscape, you have given us a brain (which contains our mind and its ability to process truth and falsehoods) that from studies we know we only use a 10th of, what is that about? Give us the courage to step out in faith and use an extra percent, if we see our results with 10%, imagine what an extra percent may bring. Help us to be suspicious, not in a bad way, but in a curious way to hunt down the truth of all matters we need to make decisions on or choose to dialogue with others on. Let "think before you speak" be our byword. In Jesus' name, we praise and thank you, Amen!

Definitions used in today's study:

Affection - from <G5424> (phren); **to exercise the mind**, i.e. **entertain or have a sentiment or opinion**; by implication **to be (mentally) disposed** (more or less earnestly in a certain direction); intensive **to interest oneself in (with concern or obedience)** :- set the affection on, (be) care (-ful), (be like-, + be of one, + be of the same, + let this) mind (-ed), regard, savour, think; probably from an obsolete phrao (to rein in or curb; compare <G5420> (phrasso)); the midrif (as a partition of the body), i.e. (figurative and by implication of sympathy) the feelings (or sensitive nature; by extension [also in the plural] the mind or cognitive faculties) :- **understanding**.

CHAPTER 3

Savoring God Knowledge

Matthew 16:23 (KJV)

23 But he turned, and said unto Peter, Get thee behind me, Satan: thou art an offence unto me: for thou savourest (exercise the mind toward, entertain, be disposed to, interest oneself in) not the things that be of God, but those that be of men.

Mark 8:33 (KJV)

33 But when he had turned about and looked on his disciples, he rebuked Peter, saying, Get thee behind me, Satan: for thou savourest (exercise the mind toward, entertain, be disposed to, interest oneself in) not the things that be of God, but the things that be of men.

Savor is the key word that we are focusing on in this part of our study about thinking and the mind. This word was translated as "affection" in the prior verse. However in these two verses, the same word is translated 'savor."

In these two accounts Jesus is rebuking the spirit of Satan working through the words of Peter. It is saying: You don't savor, you don't exercise your mind, you don't entertain, you are not mentally disposed, you don't interest yourself, you don't think of the things of God, but instead you think of things through the mind of the earthly man.

The Complete Jewish Bible translation is, "23 But Yeshua turned his back on Kefa, saying, 'Get behind me, Satan! You are an obstacle in my path, because your thinking is from a human perspective, not from God's perspective!'"

When the translators picked the word 'savor" an extra dimension was added to the meaning, that of appreciation or pleasure or enjoyment. Savor means to enjoy an experience or an activity, or feeling as much as you can and for as long as you can; taste appreciatively; or derive or receive pleasure from, get enjoyment from, take pleasure in.

This falls in line with our discussion yesterday. The key point in these two scriptures is the direction of our thoughts. No matter where we are in our walk, whether a brand new baby in Christ or a seasoned veteran, our main goal is being able to understand our relationship (interaction between people) with God through this owner's manual.

We need to clearly understand God's responsibilities and our responsibilities in order for our life to work well. Some people look at the Bible (the owner's manual) and see its close to 1500 pages and are overwhelmed. So where do we start?

Before I ever read the Bible through, I chose to watch a couple of religious programs daily, took notes and then followed up by reading the scriptures mentioned on the show. Then I wrote the verse out in my notebook and began to write about how this particular verse(s) pertained to what was happening in my life right then.

Sometimes, the link between the scripture and my life was crystal clear, but other times it was not so apparent. I used a reference Bible in the beginning and then added an Amplified Bible as time passed. In the cases where correlation didn't smack me in the face, I'd look at reference verses, read verses above and below. It wasn't long before God was talking to me about the verse and my life.

I wrote down all of my thoughts. I cringe to think of the mess that was written in those early days. However, daily new information would spark the beginning of a new understanding. Of course, everything wasn't new. Repeated themes are abundant in this Word. Repeated themes would reinforce what was studied in prior days. It wasn't long before these understandings began to compound and my thoughts, speech and actions changed day by day.

As time progressed, my favored way to study is what you see and have seen in our weekday Bible study. God impresses me through any of a dozen ways with a verse, series of verses or a topic. I then look up each word in the Strong's Concordance (and other reference tools), log those in, have a dictionary handy to translate the words within the definition (because I never cease to be amazed at what I think I know vs. what I find in that dictionary). And then I allow God to teach me.

As with any subject that we become interested in, we need continuing education. It is safe to say that when we like a subject we don't just think about it but savor the time we spend thinking about it. Conversely, there are some subjects that we may not have a great deal of interest in, but there are still reasons to pursue understanding in the subject.

You may feel that way when you begin to dig into a subject whether found in the Bible or regarding another topic that will help you make day to day decisions in other areas of your life. Some of the areas you might find you have been drifting in: your health, your weight, your style, your understanding of political issues and the law, your understanding of your rights as a citizen of the country (or state) you live in, your relationships, your emotions, statistics on your next new vehicle, science, homemaking, various business how-to's, building a world class kite, well shoot!.....you get my drift.

All of the basics are found in the Bible, and many of the particulars. But you will be required to inform yourself in the details of many other subjects to successfully maneuver in your world, to be a leader and not a sheep that can be led off a cliff. Remember! God instructs us through other texts as well as the Bible.

Good morning, Father. Thank you for helping us to see how important it is to you that we exercise our minds, not only in your principles, for without those we are severely handicapped, but also every detail required for us to operate skillfully in our lives. As we talked about yesterday, sheep we are to you, but leaders we are supposed to be to the world. The only way we can achieve this is by interest even in those things which may seem tedious and difficult to us. We need to know about the people in position who are supposed to be working for us and check up on them just as we would any employee, if they are not doing their job…we need to know and act. We need to know the details of the business venture we may be looking at so that we don't end up being a sheep lead to a financial slaughter. We need to know what chemicals are being sold and in what form to protect our families health. We pray for your direction, a hunger to learn and your direct involvement in the process of learning about the multitudes of details that only you can direct us. Give us discernment to take the next right step and to protect us from any unnecessary detours. We acknowledge, and thank you for overwhelming favor in our life and ask that you show us the people we are to help today. In Jesus' name we praise and thank you, Amen!

Definition for today's study:

Savourest / Affection - from <G5424> (phren); **to exercise the mind**, i.e. **entertain or have a sentiment or opinion**; by implication **to be (mentally) disposed** (more or less earnestly in a certain direction); intensive **to interest oneself in** (with concern or obedience) :- set the affection on, (be) care (-ful), (be like-, + be of one, + be of the same, + let this) mind (-ed), regard, **savour**, think; probably from an obsolete phrao (to rein in or curb; compare <G5420> (phrasso)); the midrif (as a partition of the body), i.e. (figurative and by implication of sympathy) the feelings (or sensitive nature; by extension [also in the plural] the mind or cognitive faculties) :- understanding.

CHAPTER 4

Informed Opinions & Responsibility

Acts 28:22 (KJV)

22 But we desire (deem entitled or fit) to hear of thee what thou thinkest (exercise the mind, have an opinion): for as concerning this sect (a party, disunion), we know that every where it is spoken against.

In this use of the word meant to "exercise the mind," Paul was addressing the Jews in Rome. He had told them that although the Romans were ready to cut him loose, the Jews (apparently a different sect from the people he was speaking with) spoke to the Roman leadership and rallied against his release. The Jews he was writing and/or speaking to wanted to know his opinion and his feelings about this situation.

They were wondering about this sect (or group of Jews) who blocked Paul's release. This seemed to be a plan or information that was not widely spread to other Jews in the region and they told Paul that they knew nothing about this.

In this case, the use of this word asks for an informed opinion from someone they trusted. Paul asked trusted associates what they had heard of his predicament and if they knew why this had happened. They responded with their ignorance of the situation.

The thing they did know was that people "everywhere" spoke against this group of people. Then they asked Paul for what his opinion or sentiment was regarding the action of the sect against him, they wanted to know his line of thinking in the matter. They trusted him.

This is how we get some of the knowledge that we gain for the operation of our lives. We piece things together from eye-witnesses to the situation. In this case Paul was the eye-witness, perhaps not to the conversation between the Roman and Jewish leadership, but certainly to the outcome of those meetings. Paul was also attempting to get some insight from the people he trusted.

I mentioned over the last couple of days that many in our world do not use this thinking process, to gain knowledge in a subject, to see if it lines up to the word of God, to practice it or put it to the test, and then once all is proven out, either add it to your repertoire or decide that this knowledge has no base in truth.

All knowledge is not truth. Wisdom can come in a flash through revelation, but generally it is a journey, it is a process to develop the proper knowledge base. Knowledge + Understanding/Experience = Wisdom. Wisdom carries with it responsibility.

Wisdom and responsibility is something we need more of. Wisdom and the knowledge it takes to get there. Whether it is Biblical knowledge, or trying to get to the bottom of why something isn't playing out according to plan in our lives, or having enough wisdom to discern and act where governmental, health, or business issues are concerned, it is our responsibility to think our way through.

Stop and think about it. Unless you are using your personal prayer language, you prayer is thought, confession of what you believe your future is takes thought, it is impossible to disconnect from it entirely. And yet, something that is not just pigeon-holed to this age, way too many people disconnect from it.

People allow others to make decisions for them, and then get angry that their life is not what it should be. They look at their situation complaining about the injustice of the climate in their life, but don't take the necessary steps to walk over to the thermostat and turn it up or down to change the climate.

I can say that I have in the past been one of these. Ticked off at the higher ups at work, or the government, or other people who seemed to have a better life than mine, blaming others for my situation instead of redirecting my thought process and gaining the necessary wisdom to change my environment.

Even within the last 2-3 years I've had to make choices between floating through or gaining more knowledge and understanding in several areas of living. Political information is one of these. I do not take anything at face value no matter which "party" it is coming from anymore.

There is more information in this arena that I do not know than what I do, but I am gaining knowledge daily. So when an issue arises or someone makes a statement, I read as much as possible on the subject, measuring it against the precepts in the Bible, I seek out opinions on all the facets available and do my best at that point to come to a stand on the issue at hand.

It is important as a citizen to know more. We need to know both history and current events. What we don't know we need to take an active part in learning. The same can be said for many subjects that affect our individual lives.

It is also to our benefit to withhold our opinions when we do not know the facts of a matter. When we have only taken the word of one person and run with it as our own, we are unable to intelligently carry on a discussion with an informed party. Holding back until we know more and have time to think it over is part of being responsible.

Sometimes we will have to admit our lack of knowledge. Admitting our ignorance in a subject will gain more respect than our spouting out someone else's opinion and not being able to back it up. In our businesses, a lack of knowledge can be purchased through hiring a person who knows the field (I.T., Accounting, Production, Marketing, etc.). However, if you hire the wrong "expert" your business could be in trouble.

My point is our responsibility is wider than we may have originally thought. And if you come to this party late, as I did in many areas, the task of understanding can seem daunting. This is where having a solid base of knowledge in Biblical principles comes to play.

Having this gives us a "truth" filter that will help us screen information according to how God says it should be. The Holy Spirit will nudge us when something "just doesn't seem right." Then we can take time to do a little research, including prayer before we respond openly.

Our relationship with the Father/Son/Holy Spirit gives us the plus that will move us ahead more quickly at any task that seems daunting. I am not asking you to do anything God has not. In Matthew 13:12 For whosoever hath, to him shall be given, and he shall have more abundance, but whosoever hath not, from him shall be taken away even that he hath. Diligence is so important; it is key.

Good morning, Father. Thank you for the "plus" our relationship gives when we choose to take responsibility for our life instead of allowing others to do our thinking for us. Although we may right now see several areas of our life where we have allowed this to happen, help us to focus on one of these areas and guide us through becoming disciplined to gain the knowledge needed to make wise decisions, to filter information coming to us from outside sources, and knowing when we are to voice opinions (based in your truth and facts of the matter) and when we are to remain silent. In all of this we know that some feathers may be ruffled; we need both wisdom and courage to walk through this also. We thank you for the Holy Spirit's discernment to alert us to incorrect information, and the discipline to gather facts of the subject before we act or speak. In all this, we thank you for your grace that is fully operational in all areas of our life. As we choose responsibility over drifting, we know you are backing us. Help us to see where we can help and the resources to do so. In Jesus' name, we praise and thank you, Amen!

Thinkest / Savourest / Affection - from <G5424> (phren); **to exercise the mind**, i.e. **entertain or have a sentiment or opinion**; by implication **to be (mentally) disposed** (more or less earnestly in a certain direction); intensive **to interest oneself in** (with concern or obedience) :- set the affection on, (be) care (-ful), (be like-, + be of one, + be of the same, + let this) mind (-ed), regard, **savour**, think; probably from an obsolete phrao (to rein in or curb; compare <G5420> (phrasso)); the midrif (as a partition of the body), i.e. (figurative and by implication of sympathy) the feelings (or sensitive nature; by extension [also in the plural] the mind or cognitive faculties) :- understanding

CHAPTER 5

Extreme Makeover, Living Life

Romans 12:2 (KJV)

2 And be not (qualified negation) conformed (to fashion alike, make in an image like, in its pattern) to this world (an age, course): but be ye transformed (have a completely different form or appearance) by the **renewing** (renovation, act of restoring to its former good condition) of your mind (the intellect: creative use of mind, ability to understand complicated subjects), that ye may prove what is that good, and acceptable, and perfect, will of God.

I was having a conversation with a friend over the weekend and she mentioned the difference in our society today compared to that when we were growing up. Back then there were some things that were taboo, some things just not said or done in polite company.

Verbalizing even a couple of the lesser evil cuss words was considered the height of naughtiness, and the hard core cuss words were appalling. Most of the time these words were not used in mixed company. Men might say these things when together, but a gentleman did not say these things in front of women, especially single women that they might have a romantic interest in.

They may loosen up once married (and the wife usually corrected this “bad behavior”), but before then it was just not considered appropriate. Little by little over the last 45-50 years women began to slide into using foul language and in many cases every bit as often as men. Perhaps, for women, it was that in the workplace they would be heard if they cussed, or as they more frequently went out on the town that loose language was part of the ebb and flow of conversation oiled up by drink.

One of the primary steps in creating a Godly lifestyle is, to use your mouth to speak God's desires over you and your family. So it makes sense that the using negative words of the world will degrade society. A massive change in society has occurred through our speech becoming so loose, and this goes hand in hand with thinking. Speaking is an action, as well as other physical actions and they are initiated by the thought process.

As you can see our society’s thoughts have strayed far from the thoughts of God. At one time in history, and not so long ago and even if they were not church goers, most everyone was aware of the Ten Commandments. Everyone knew instinctively it was wrong to steal, to take the Lord’s name in vain, not to go to church, to not honor your dad and mom, to kill, to have sex with someone prior to marriage or with someone who was married to someone else, to lie, or to covet.

Usually even non-church goers knew these eight of the Ten. People somehow believed that God was keeping an eye on them and their life through their following these guidelines to right living (or not). And although most people were at least partially contained by worry that God would throw a lightning bolt their way if they messed up, still there were those who cast all care to the wind and lived as crazy as they wanted.

Don't misunderstand me. Back then all wasn't sunshine and roses, but people showed some restraint by having these boundaries out in the public eye. In self-sufficiency there was personal responsibility and dignity. Much has changed over the years however; we have the ability to change our life back toward a more Godly way. It begins in our own life. Changing our thought begins the process and ripples outward into the world at large.

This verse is telling us that with qualified negation we are not to be conformed to the pattern of this age. The dictionary definition of negation is the act of saying no, the fact that something is made to have no effect, the speech act of negating and/or a negative statement; a statement that is a refusal or denial of some other statement.

Negation is in essence drawing a boundary, a boundary to keep out "God contrary" thoughts, words and deeds. The dictionary definition of qualified is: limited or restricted; not absolute. Here is where thinking about something rather than just reading it is important. It is a qualifying statement and means that our saying "no" to the things of the age or course of things which are not absolute.

In my mind's eye, it is saying we need to say "no" to trends, ideas, and mores that don't align with God. However, there are natural laws of this world that are God solid and absolute. For us to attempt to negate an absolute natural law would cause us harm (i.e. Gravity).

Instead of conforming to current social mores, continued study and prayer give our life a completely different appearance than what was seen previously. Changes for the better occur when our mind and heart line up with God, his precepts and principles, and take our proper place in our relationship with Him.

If we do not use our thought process to investigate our place in this relationship we will continue to fall back on relying on ourselves rather than believing He has his part and we ours. With our investigation, thought (meditation or mulling it over and over) and prayer, changes occur in our heart and mind that change our appearance to the world.

Good morning, Father. Thank you for showing us that as we start at home, with ourselves as our first project, every step we take in the right direction makes a difference in the world. Many of us come to you with a life that is near unbearable, but have been searching for the way out of a mess. The more we know you and change because of this renewing we find higher levels to walk with you. We know our change is never done. Some of the early changes will be most apparent outwardly, like an extreme makeover, and as time goes by many of the changes will be not so outwardly evident. These will be changes between you and us, all at heart level. This is a manifestation of 2 Corinthians 3:18 that we "…are changed into the same image from glory to glory". Give us a desire that outweighs the problems to find the answers we need. Your Book is our owner's manual with what sometimes appears to be contradictory information, but oftentimes these things are not contradictions but instead we are holding the puzzle piece upside-down or side-ways, with you in our quiet time you will show us how it needs to be turned to fit, as soon as it happens, other things begin to fall into place in our lives. You graciously provide us with a covering of favor that others see. Thank you for showing us those we are to be of service to today. In Jesus' name, we praise and thank you, Amen!

Definitions for today's study:

Not – a primary particle of **qualified negation**

Conformed - from <G4862> (sun) and a derivative of <G4976> (schema); to **fashion alike**, i.e. **conform to the same pattern** (figurative) :- conform to, fashion self according to; a primary preposition **denoting union**; with or together (but much closer than <G3326> (meta) or <G3844> (para)), i.e. by association, companionship, process, **resemblance**, possession, instrumentality, addition, etc. :- beside, with. In comparative it has similar applications, including completeness.

World – from the same as <G104> (aei); properly **an age**; by extension **perpetuity (also past)**; by implication the world; specially (Jewish) a Messianic period (present or future) :- age, course, eternal, (for) ever (-more), [n-]ever, (beginning of the, while the) world (began, without end). Compare <G5550> (chronos).

Transformed - from <G3326> (meta) and <G3445> (morphoo); to transform (literal or figurative "metamorphose") :- **change**, transfigure, transform; from <G3326> (meta) and <G3445> (morphoo); to transform (literal or figurative "metamorphose") :- change, transfigure, transform.; a division or share.

Renewing - from <G341> (anakainoo); **renovation** :- renewing; from <G303> (ana) and a derivative of <G2537> (kainos); to renovate :- renew; a primary preposition and adverb; properly up; but (by extension) used (distributively) severally, or (locally) at (etc.) :- and, apiece, by, each, every (man), in, through. In compounds (as a prefix) it often means (by implication) repetition, intensity, reversal, etc.

Mind - probably from the base of <G1097> (ginosko); **the *intellect [creative use of the mind, ability to understand***

difficult or complicated subjects], i.e. ***mind* (divine or human; in thought, feeling, or will)**; by implication *meaning* :- mind, understanding. Compare <G5590> (psuche); a prolonged form of a primary verb; to "know" (absolute), in a great variety of applications and with many implication (as follow, with others not thus clearly expressed) :- allow, be aware (of), feel, (have) know (-ledge), perceive, be resolved, can speak, **be sure**, understand

CHAPTER 6

On Purpose Thinking

Romans 12:2 (KJV)

2 And be not conformed to this world: but be ye transformed by the **renewing** of your mind (the intellect: creative use of mind, ability to understand complicated subjects), that ye may prove (to test, to approve, discern [to notice something, especially after thinking about it carefully or studying it]) what is that good, and acceptable, and perfect, will of God.

Yesterday we spoke of renewing the mind, basically the idea that our mind is to be restored to God's original design. The second part of the verse tells us why.

Until you look closely at the words in this verse, it is not evident that there are two references to thinking and the mind, not one. "Mind" is used in the first portion, and the word used in the second portion has to do with using mental capabilities is "prove." This is an "on purpose" thinking, disciplined thought, focused thought.

The main definition for "prove" is to test. Testing something is to discerning that there is validity to the statement, principle or application. Many people in the church act as though discernment is something that happens through the senses, some floaty, sometimes scary, other-worldly thing that happens and that it is for some people but not all.

They look at discernment as ethereal, like this dictionary definition "as impalpable or intangible as air." But if that were the case why would God have this as an instruction for all of us? He told us to regenerate, refresh, renew our minds. We are to change our mind from "God contrary' thinking.

God is nothing but true and practical. It is amazing how much we can obtain by quickly reading the scripture and even through someone else's training. Nuggets that help us be better and have better for our lives. But from this verse we can see he has more for those who will follow through on this instruction.

God is gracious and knows that many will not take the time to dig, however from this part of the verse it is what he is asking us to do. From the definition of "discern" we see that it is to notice something, especially after thinking about it carefully or studying it.

Let me present this thought, there are things that we just have to take at face value and in faith in the beginning. This beginning could be when you are a babe in Christ or it could be the beginning of a new level of understanding. However it becomes clearer, as we go along in our study that his desire is for us to dig deeper using our head for more than a hat rack.

I am not relegating this behavior strictly to Biblical studies, and do not believe God is either. We are to prove the good, acceptable and perfect (complete, in various applications of labor, growth, mental and moral character) will (preferred or chosen way) for our lives. This part of the phrase is not only about the Biblical but shows regard for all areas concerning our life.

Good morning, Father. Thank you for helping us to see your will or as the definition proves out to us "your chosen way," "your preferred way" in all areas of our life. This covers our moral life, and without a steady moral compass the other areas of our lives are tainted. Gratefully our "plus" is knowing You and the grace you favor us with. In our relationship, we gain friendship, protection, love that we can find nowhere else. There is not enough "thanks" for these. Many are lost and hurting and need what you so lavishly give to us, help us to show You to them through our lives. You are the light in us that draws them in. In Jesus' name, we praise and thank you, Amen!

Definitions for today's study:

Prove - from <G1384> (dokimos); **to test** (literal or figurative); by implication **to approve** :- **allow**, **discern [to notice something, especially after thinking about it carefully or studying it]**, **examine**, × like, (ap-) prove, try; from <G1380> (dokeo); properly acceptable (current after assayal), i.e. approved :- approved, tried; a prolonged form of a primary verb doko, dok"-o (used only as an alternate in certain tenses; compare the base of <G1166> (deiknuo)) of the same meaning; **to think**; by implication to seem (truthfully or uncertainly) :- be accounted, (of own) please (-ure), be of reputation, seem (good), suppose, think, trow.

Acceptable - from <G2095> (eu) and <G701> (arestos); **fully agreeable** :- acceptable (-ted), wellpleasing; neuter of a primary eus (good); (adverb) well :- good, well (done) + from <G700>

(aresko); agreeable; by implication fit :- (things that) please (-ing), reason; probably from <G142> (airo) (through the idea of exciting emotion); to be agreeable (or by implication to seek to be so) :- please; a primary verb; to lift; by implication to take up or away; figurative to raise (the voice), keep in suspense (the mind); specially to sail away (i.e. weigh anchor); by Hebrew [compare <H5375> (nasa")] to expiate sin :- away with, bear (up), carry, lift up, loose, make to doubt, put away, remove, take (away, up).

Perfect - from <G5056> (telos); **complete** (in various applications of labor, growth, mental and moral character, etc.); neuter (as noun, with <G3588> (ho)) completeness :- of full age, man, perfect; from a primary tello (to set out for a definite point or goal); properly the point aimed at as a limit, i.e. (by implication) the conclusion of an act or state (termination [literal, figurative or indefinite], result [immediate, ultimate or prophetic], purpose); specially an impost or levy (as paid) :- + continual, custom, end (-ing), finally, uttermost.

Will - from the prolonged form of <G2309> (thelo); **a determination** (properly the thing), i.e. (active) choice (special purpose, decree; abstract volition) or (passive) inclination :- desire, pleasure, will; or ethelo, eth-el"-o; in certain tenses theleo, thel-eh"-o; and etheleo, eth-el-eh"-o, which are otherwise obsolete; apparently strengthened from the altnate form of <G138> (haireomai); to determine (as an active option from subjective impulse; whereas <G1014> (boulomai) properly denotes rather a passive acquiescence in objective considerations), i.e., **choose or prefer** (literal or figurative); by implication to wish, i.e. be inclined to (sometimes adverbially gladly); impersonally for the future tense, to be about to; by Hebrew to delight in :- desire, be disposed (forward), intend, list, love, mean, please, have rather, (be) will (have, -ling, -ling [ly]).

CHAPTER 7

Thoughts Flavor Your Day

Joshua 1:8 (KJV)

8 This book of the law shall not depart out of thy mouth; but thou shalt meditate therein day and night, that thou mayest observe to do according to all that is written therein: for then thou shalt make thy way prosperous, and then thou shalt have good success.

For those of you who have followed our blog posts, earlier this year we did a study on Joshua 1:3-9. The focus for the breakdown of verse :8 was on the mouth and meditation (the thought process). The connection is clear. God is speaking to Joshua with a message for him and the people he was now charged with leading into the Promised Land.

His promise was that every place the sole of their foot landed would be theirs, he spoke of a particular land with some beach front property (this was important not only in the aspect of the beauty of such a spot but also because of commerce, very important for their prosperity prospects), the guarantee that other men would not be able to stand before them (they would come out on top), and then he says "be of good courage". To make this statement indicates a foreknowledge of some threat that they would be facing while taking possession of this promise.

'Courage' a primitive root; to be alert, physically (on foot) or mentally (in courage):- confirm, be courageous (of good courage, **steadfastly minded**, strong, stronger), establish, fortify, harden, increase, prevail, strengthen (self), make strong (**obstinate [not willing to be reasonable and change your plans, ideas, or behavior]**, speed) [Strong's Concordance].

Courage speaks of a strong or steadfast mind. This is what we are pointing to in our discussion of thinking for ourselves, being informed thinkers. Our goal is to be focused, determined and disciplined thinkers.

The verse tells us to be strong, obstinate. When measuring situations and plans and people to Biblical principles, we are to be unwilling to change our plans, ideas or behavior in regard to our understanding of these principles and precepts. So what is the threat?

Wrong thinking in the face of problems, weak or vacillating thought that keeps us hopping from one side of the issue to the other. Our greatest threat is simply not thinking of what God has said about a particular situation and in this lack of action, becoming a sheep following someone else's plan for our lives.

By keeping the precepts and principles of God's perfect life design in our mouth, by actively choosing to discuss them with family, friends and associates as the opportunity arises, we increase our understanding and belief in them.

It may not occur to us at first glance, but thinking and speaking and acting are interconnected. You find this in the definitions of the words. Keeping this in mind, one of the words that is used in Strong's Concordance to define the word "mouth", is "mind". The word translated "meditate" has words like "murmur, speak, talk and utter" as well as the thinking aspect within the definition.

When I think of meditation I still have in mind the person sitting cross-legged, hands with palms up, middle finger and thumb touching. I am not trying to be flip; however the point is that most people don't really meditate like this. However through repetitively seeing this in conjunction with the word 'meditate', it is seen as the universal pose when meditating. We see here that meditating is something different.

There is a distinct connection between thinking and speaking. The more you think of something, the more the flavor of those thoughts find their way out in the words you speak and the tone in which you speak them. Speaking is a powerful tool that we do not use to its full benefit.

If we were taught as children the importance of diligence in thought and speech, we would be miles ahead. But because this is not done, we lazily allow way too many thoughts and words to flow through our mind and mouth unwatched.

Even knowing the positive changes that have occurred in my life through following this instruction, I still find that unless I discipline myself to do it, it won't happen. I can remain silent or speak contrary without discipline.

It says that it is not just about reading it. Instead, it clearly states that by speaking and meditating on its contents you will make your way prosperous and have good success.

Any of you who have known me for more than a minute or two know that I have developed daily affirmations or declarations or confessions, whichever term you choose to use for years. This verse was written way back when, and the way that they kept these laws in their mouths was through the telling around the fire at night, at a noon day meal and in their morning prayer.

We can do this in very similar ways. I really can't explain the inner workings of this, but I can tell you that when you continue to speak or murmur (not just think, mull over) what God has said about you it strengthens your belief that you are to have God's best. Somehow meditating and speaking aloud His word, can and does transform little by little natural circumstances and situations.

Even meditation here means murmur (to saying something in a very low voice), imagine, ponder, mutter, speak, study, or muse (think slowly). In our definition of the word "musing" we see "a calm, lengthy, and intent consideration" and "being persistently thoughtful".

The corresponding benefit to speaking and meditating on this is that you will make your way prosperous and have good success. He wants this for you and you should too.

This word translated as "prosperous" means to push forward, break out, come mightily, be good, or be profitable. And the word translated "good success" is the exact same word used in the previous verse that translated out as prosper. The base elements of this word include; intelligence, understanding and wisdom. Wisdom seems to control a flow of all aspects of a prosperous life.

Tomorrow we will take a quick look at another of the definitions of meditate.

Good morning, Father. Thank you for this wonderful powerhouse we call the brain, the unseen mind and its ability to process millions and millions of pieces of information throughout the course of every day. We ask that you help us to access and utilize to a greater extent this gift. We may not see ourselves on the same level as an Einstein, but what about a Ford, an Edison, a Gates, a Getty, a Mother Theresa or Gandhi or Mandela, what about a Franklin or Jefferson or Washington? Each of these made historic contributions to this country and the world. I believe that is what you would like for us. Thank you for the desire to find and make our unique contribution to mankind. In Jesus' name, we praise and thank you for it....Amen!

Definitions use in today's study:

Mouth - from <H6284> (pa'ah); the mouth (as the means of blowing), whether literal or figurative (particularly speech); specifically edge, portion or side; adverbially (with preposition) according to :- accord (-ing as, -ing to), after, appointment, assent, collar, command (-ment), × eat, edge, end, entry, + file, hole, × in, **mind**, mouth, part, portion, × (should) say (-ing), sentence, **skirt**, sound, speech, × spoken, talk, tenor, × to, + two-edged, wish, word; a primitive root; to puff, i.e. blow away :- scatter into corners.

Meditate - a primitive root [compare <H1901> (hagiyg)]; **to murmur** (in pleasure or anger); by implication **to ponder** :- **imagine**, **meditate**, mourn, mutter, roar, × sore, speak, study, talk, utter; from an unused root akin to <H1897> (hagah);

properly a murmur, i.e. complaint :- meditation, **<u>musing (persistently thoughtful, a calm lengthy intent consideration).</u>**

CHAPTER 8

Unpleasant Situation? Skirt the Issue!

Joshua 1:8 (KJV)

8 This book of the law shall not depart out of thy mouth (skirt); but thou shalt meditate therein day and night, that thou mayest observe to do according to all that is written therein: for then thou shalt make thy way prosperous, and then thou shalt have good success.

I misspoke yesterday when I mentioned that today we would look at another of the definitions for "meditate," it is really from the word translated "mouth." And the word "skirt." the descriptor I found so fascinating. What could skirt have to do with the mouth and meditation? Let's look at what a skirt means:

- A dress, or coat that is below the waist

- Something that covers the lower part of a machine or vehicle

- To go around the edge of a place or thing, move along the border

- To avoid talking about something unpleasant

- Avoid fulfilling, answering or performing duties, questions or issues

In my 20+ years of using this verse as part of my confession, I have never until two days ago seen this. I remember a teaching by Rabbi Lapin that said (and this is paraphrasing), if when you look at the definition of a Hebrew word and you see something that doesn't seem to fit, there is always a connection in the message. Hopefully we can catch a glimpse of it here.

The first purpose of a skirt (as a garment or accessory) is that of protection. A skirt whether part of a piece of clothing or metal frame at the base of a piece of equipment, provides a boundary of sorts. It protects the objects underneath. It can be protection from intrusion by elements that could harm, or protection from those things that were meant by the designer of that equipment (whether it is a human or a machine) to be of a private nature.

The second purpose of a skirt is to decoratively hide the mechanics (or productive part) of a thing. Again a kind of protection, because not always is the inner workings of a thing pretty to eyes other than those of the designers. The inner working of a person or a machine is the place where the power of production happens. This could be a reproduction as in the case of having children, or production of an idea, business or goods.

Could it be that the hidden meaning of this is that by learning the precepts and principles of God and keeping them in our mind for emergency situations that they are building what we see called in other areas of the Bible a "hedge of protection" for all productive areas of our life?

Is this a hedge that protects the private areas of our lives not only from outside intruders but prying, niggling thoughts about our own past, those thoughts meant to entrap us in the past to keep us from our rightful future? We can look at this as a boundary (this skirt or these words) that has more spiritual latitude than we perceive at a first glance, a spiritual boundary that our enemies have a particularly difficult time stepping foot across.

The second purpose of the skirt as a decorative covering makes the idea of speaking the word over our lives like a beautifully colored fabric covering our legs (the symbolic means for us moving forward to success). Speaking God's words are that beautiful fabric covering the mechanics of how we are going to get where we are going, how we are going to be prosperous and have good success.

Stop and think about all the people you know that keep walking day by day though their lives, taking the next right step and going in a direction toward a goal they call "X." The next thing you know, the real success they find is a place God had for them all the time, a different spot even more beautiful.

If you talk to this successful person they may say, "I never believed that I'd be doing this," or "This is so much better than I ever thought it could be." When you get down to how it happened, it came by what seemed to be serendipitous event or series of events. As we don't believe in luck or coincidence, we have to believe that God has used this 'skirt" to hide the extent of his plan for us.

He gave us some knowledge of the dream, but not the path. He hid this in order to arrange things for us that we had no idea were even possible.

The words we speak in confession (a part of this skirt) are often so grand that they are near unbelievable for the mind of a person who has grown up being programmed in defeat, poverty, and victim mentality. You might feel that just because you are you, there is some hidden agenda by the higher-ups to keep you squashed down, poor you, there is just nothing you can do about it. Well, all that thinking is wrong! By speaking the words of God, these new thoughts overcome and vanquish years of bad programming.

Now there is one other aspect of the definition of skirt, and that is the idea of choosing not to talk about something because it is unpleasant or to avoid issues by not answering questions or performing duties responsibly.

In essence when we speak God's word instead of the problem in front of us or the circumstance that doesn't measure up to God's best for us, we may be seen by others in our circle to be delusional. We may seem to be avoiding responsibility, or just a dreamer who doesn't want to talk about unpleasant things.

This is where an understanding of who we are and our relationship with the Almighty comes into play. This whole study regarding thinking properly is about moving from being a person who floats along in life to one who is deliberately thinking, side by side with God.

Unfortunately by the time we wake up from our "sleep" and recognize that there is something better out there for us, oftentimes our life is a mess and looks like the complete opposite of the original plan. So in these cases (and this can be a fractional difference or a massive chasm), by "skirting" those issues with God's word, He is able to work behind the scenes lining things up for a change. I'm ready! How about you?

Good morning, Father. Thank you for pointing out small details that don't seem to fit, and for giving us the desire to look at their meaning. By speaking Your word, more is released than the words themselves. These words are keys that unlock secret workings of plans you have had for us through the ages, these words protect us from negative thoughts that attempt to hold us back, they create a spiritual boundary that our enemies have a hard time stepping over and protect the most private and productive parts of our being. You can then operate in our life in ways that, as our Daddy, you have always wanted to and we have not given full permission. We open ourselves today to receiving every good thing from you, not only for ourselves but for those you place in our path. In Jesus' name, we praise and thank you, Amen!

Definitions use in today's study:

Mouth - from <H6284> (pa"ah); the mouth (as the means of blowing), whether literal or figurative (particularly speech); specifically edge, portion or side; adverbially (with preposition) according to :- accord (-ing as, -ing to), after, appointment, assent, collar, command (-ment), × eat, edge, end, entry, + file, hole, × in, **mind**, mouth, part, portion, × (should) say (-ing), sentence, **skirt**, sound, speech, × spoken, talk, tenor, × to, + two-edged, wish, word; a primitive root; to puff, i.e. blow away :- scatter into corners.

CHAPTER 9

The Evil Eye & Food for Thought

Proverbs 23:6 (KJV)

6 Eat (<u>feed on, set all your attention on, interest</u>) thou not the bread (<u>food</u>) of him that hath an evil eye (discernment, clever idea, subject), neither desire (<u>have in mind</u>) thou his dainty meats (<u>to perceive</u>):

I began to study the verse "As a man thinks in his heart, so is he," but as always I read above and below, and found that there is a reason that this statement was made. As you may know this does not always happen in Proverbs like other chapters where a story line is often found. But this is well worth mentioning and making a part of our study.

This verse has as much to do with not getting used to hanging out with wrong people and eating a rare or expensive type of food as is does with a state of mind that goes along with this. First looking at the word "eat" and "bread" we see that it too has a dual meaning.

This word can mean just what it says, the act of eating food, however the dictionary says it can mean something that causes anxiety or worry. As in "don't let this thing eat away at you." Worry is a thinking process.

The Strong's Concordance uses words like consume, which can mean eating or it can mean taking all your attention. This thing takes up so much of your brain space that you cannot think of anything else. Attention is a thinking process. It can also mean devour which can mean eat food or to enjoy with interest. Both "enjoy" and "interest" are thinking processes.

Thinking and the state of mind in which we go into our relationships and business ventures have everything to do with the "food," the material or ideas we choose to bring (or allow) into our mind.

Stop and think of the good kid who is living in a constant state of want. He goes to church with his mom, but his dad is not an everyday influence in his life. Mom is an upright and decent person. She knows what she would like for her children and through one of the many reasons people do not stay together she and her husband separated early in her child's life.

When this happened, a part of her left with him and try as she might she cannot give her son what he needs and would have gotten from having his father in the home. She works two jobs attempting to make ends meet, and although she does have a roof over their head and food on the table it is not all she would like to give.

He goes to school and sees that others have (or seem to have) much that he does not. One of his buddies, you know one of the ones his mom wouldn't be happy about him hanging with, begins to whisper in his ear that he has just met this group of guys. Hey why don't you come down and have some dinner with us while your mom is at her second job.

He goes, and this isn't just a burger, it is a steak with all the fixings, drink and dessert. He's heard of it but never experienced it. They joke with him and make him feel at home. Pretty soon he is spending more time with them, less time at home. Mom senses the changes and feels her son slipping away. It isn't long before he is out there on the street, doing what he is doing and in trouble up to his eyeballs.

Well, this doesn't just happen to children, if you have had an area of lack in your life there is a chink in your armor that gives evil an opening to slide in. This could be a real or perceived lack.

In my books, I mention this aspect often, because we often get into a mess when we perceive a lack, or that a slight that has been committed against us. It is a wrong thinking process, a misinterpretation of facts.

Adults get in business deals that sour or were destined to fail from the beginning because they felt it would supply some need. They chose to act before they took an opportunity to gather and mull over all the facts.

I'd like to say that it all started with a fancy meal and some laughs, whether we are talking about that little story I related about the youth or with the adult who got into a bad business deal, an abusive relationship, or even that person who is susceptible to being overweight and thinks it is okay to eat two tasty deserts every day and not pay the consequences.

But it is a state of mind, a thought process that something is missing, and you have to try to fill that need yourself. The food is an inroad, whether physical food or mental food.

The type of food or thought is the problem. What are you choosing to chew on? Are your thoughts Godly food? …or, are you believing you are in want? …or, are you believing that things won't get better, and you don't have a choice? One type of food or thought or perception is that of lack and want. The other is of hope and faith. Chew on that.

Good morning, Father. Thank you for helping us to be more aware of the type of food we put in our minds and bodies. We could choose the bitter food of lack, want, worry and anxiety, all leading to weakness. Or we could choose the sweet food of hope and faith and strength. We choose strength today. It never ceases to amaze, the way you have arranged the words in your text to tell a story so that we can clearly understand. Always I felt that this verse was about the thinking aspect of life, you prove it out to us by the definitions of words we never would normally associate with the thought process. Open our eyes to see more, and how we can apply this to our life today. Give us wisdom, wisdom that when applied will benefit us and others in our circle. In Jesus' name, we praise and thank you, Amen!

Definitions used in today's study:

Eat - a primitive root; **to feed on**; figurative to **consume [to take all of your attention so that you cannot think of anything else, engage fully]**; by implication to battle (as destruction) :- **devour [enjoy avidly, to read, watch, or listen to something with a lot of interest or enthusiasm]**, eat, × ever, fight (-ing), overcome, prevail, (make) war (-ring).

Bread - from <H3898> (lacham); **food** (for man or beast), especially bread, or grain (for making it) :- ([shew-]) bread, × eat, food, fruit, loaf, meat, victuals. See also <H1036> (Beyth le-

`Aphrah); a primitive root; to feed on; figurative to consume; by implication to battle (as destruction) :- devour, eat, × ever, fight (-ing), overcome, prevail, (make) war (-ring).

Evil - from <H7489> (ra`a`); bad or (as noun) evil (natural or moral) :- adversity, affliction, bad, calamity, + displease (-ure), distress, evil ([-favouredness], man, thing), + exceedingly, × great, grief (-vous), harm, heavy, hurt (-ful), ill (favoured), + mark, mischief (-vous), misery, naught (-ty), noisome, + not please, sad (-ly), sore, sorrow, trouble, vex, wicked (-ly, -ness, one), worse (-st), wretchedness, wrong. [Incling feminine ra`ah; as adjective or noun.]; a primitive root; properly to spoil (literal by breaking to pieces); figurative to make (or be) good for nothing, i.e. bad (physically, socially or morally) :- afflict, associate selves [by mistake for <H7462> (ra`ah)], break (down, in pieces), + displease, (be, bring, do) evil (doer, entreat, man), show self friendly [by mistake for <H7462> (ra`ah)], do harm, (do) hurt, (behave self, deal) ill, × indeed, do mischief, punish, still, vex, (do) wicked (doer, -ly), be (deal, do) worse.

Eye - probably a primitive word; an **eye [good discernment (either with the eyes or as if with the eyes)]** (literal or figurative); by analogy a fountain (as the eye of the landscape) :- affliction, outward appearance, + before, + think best, colour, **conceit [a clever and unusual idea or way of comparing things]**, + be **content [the subject, ideas, or story that a piece of writing]**, countenance, + displease, eye ([brow], [-d], -sight), face, + favour, fountain, furrow [from the margin], × him, + humble, knowledge, look, (+ well), × me, open (-ly), + (not) please, presence, + regard, resemblance, sight, × thee, × them, + think, × us, well, × you (-rselves).

Desire - a primitive root; **to wish for [have in mind]**:- covet, (greatly) desire, be desirous, long, lust (after).

Dainty meats - or (feminine) mat`ammah, mat-am-maw"; from <H2938> (ta`am); a delicacy :- dainty (meat), savoury meat; a primitive root; to *taste*; figurative ***to perceive*** :- × but, perceive, taste.

CHAPTER 10

Completely Unhinged & Sloppy Living

Proverbs 23:7

For as he thinketh (to split open, act as gate-keeper, estimate, use or exercise the mind) in his heart, so is he,

In yesterday's study the verse stated that food is an inroad to our thought processes, and that eventually these thoughts translate to speech and other physical actions. This can be either physical food to fuel your body, or food that has been misused to the point of making the abuser overweight or obese.

It can be mental food too. Just as physical food comforts us, is a centerpiece of celebration and is necessary for a properly functioning body. Mental food hits us on near every level as food for the body except, where a plate of green salad and chicken fuels the body for the next few hours, mental food feeds and fuels our intellect, our spirit and emotions for days weeks and even years.

Physical food can be abused. Admittedly I have been an offender in this area. Mental food can also be abused. For years I took my lead in the mental food area from the great "they", .instead of the great "I Am." In the last few years my eyes have been opened to this and I have made changes. From all I've seen, a myriad of people out there are facing this same dilemma. Good people, misled.

The word "thinketh" means to split open like a two sectioned gate and to exercise the mind. We are to treat our thinking like a gate, a gate that we regulate. Gates are usually attached to a fence. We can look at this fence as a boundary. Boundaries keep outside influences from your property, lawn, garden and home, your business, your family, your emotional, mental and spiritual self.

Expanded outward, fences (or walls) surrounded cities to keep out uninvited travelers, neighbors and warring forces throughout history. Food for thought comes to us in too many forms to be listed here. We have more than 48 thoughts per minute according to some studies. That is 70,000 thoughts per day.

It doesn't take us looking at the world at large, but just a look at our own backyard to know that most people have a fence around their figurative yard however the gate is wide open. I think it would be safe to say that the gate is cast sideways, dangling by one hinge. And in many cases the gate is lying on the ground, completely unhinged.

Keeping your mind safe by keeping the gate in good repair and making sure that it was secured when not allowing someone (thought) in, was not something that was taught to us as children. So it is as though this hoard of thoughts is assailing the gate with a broken latch, before long you find that the gate is non-existent, and your mind has becoming the playground of warring factions.

These unruly and unwanted visitors are other people's thoughts and opinions, half-truths or no truths trampling on core values, or worse. When people don't have established core values as an anchor, it is easier to have these ungodly precepts gain ground. These folks act a chameleon and in attempting to fit in they change to fit the crowd they are currently with.

We are to act as a gate-keeper, a porter over the property of our mind. A porter is a person employed to carry luggage and supplies (the thoughts and values formed by those thoughts necessary for productive living); someone who guards an entrance (choosing which thoughts will propel you into the future or keep you bogged down in the past); or someone in a station, airport, or hotel whose job is helping people with their suitcases and showing them where to go (guiding your life through solid, directed and focused thought).

So the choice is ours. Will we choose to hide in our mental house afraid of taking a stand, or worse yet be tossed from one side to the other by someone else's opinions and distorted truths? Or...Do we choose to stand guard over the gate of our mind? Will we stand there with a figurative clipboard and measure thoughts against God based precepts and principles? The choice is ours.

Good morning, Father. Thank you for showing us the inner workings of why we are where we are in our journey. In some cases, our gate is completely unhinged, and in this area our life looks to the outside observer as sloppy. Thank you for showing us that the answer is simple, when we change our thoughts and we change our world. Now a simple concept doesn't necessarily mean easy to do. In one way or another we have been programmed from childhood with "stuff" that is counterproductive to living well. Each of us may have a different area of struggle, and maybe until today we didn't even realize we had the problem or that there was something we could do to combat it. We ask for insight as to what area is our current and most active problem, then help us to replace the hinges on that gate, and with a clipboard in hand stand guard mentally over thoughts that are contrary to the promise you have given us in that area. Each minute we are able to effectively stand guard, strengthens us and makes the way easier. We choose to receive your grace and favor to overcome whatever intruder we have wrestled with and slam the gate "locked" behind him. In Jesus' name, we praise and thank you, Amen!

Definitions used in today's study:

Thinks - a primitive root; **to split or open**, i.e. (literal, but only as denominative from <H8179> (sha`ar)) **to act as gate-keeper** (see <H7778> (show`er)); (figurative) **to estimate [to say what you think an amount or value will be, either by guessing or by using available information to calculate it]**:- **think [use or exercise the mind or one's power of reason in order to make inferences, decisions, or arrive at a solution or judgments]**; from <H8176> (sha`ar) **in its original sense; an opening**, i.e. door or gate :- city, door, gate, port (× -er); or sho`er, sho-are"; active participle of <H8176> (sha`ar) (as denominative from <H8179> (sha`ar)); a janitor :- door-keeper, **porter**.

Heart - from <H5314> (naphash); properly **a breathing creature**, i.e. animal or (abstract) **vitality**; used very widely in a literal, accommodated or figurative sense (**bodily or mental**) :- any, **appetite [a feeling of being very interested in something]**, beast, body, **breath**, creature, × dead (-ly), desire, × [dis-] **contented**, × fish, ghost, + greedy, he, heart (-y), (hath, ×

jeopardy of) **life** (× in jeopardy), **lust**, man, **me**, **mind**, mortally, one, own, person, pleasure, (her-, him-, my-, thy-) self, them (your) -selves, + slay, **soul**, + tablet, they, thing, (× she) will, × would have it; a primitive root; to breathe; passive, to be breathed upon, i.e. (figurative) refreshed (as if by a current of air) :- (be) refresh selves (-ed).

CHAPTER 11

Guarded Access, Layers of Security

Ezekiel 38:10-12 (KJV)

10 Thus saith the Lord GOD; It shall also come to pass, that at the same time shall things come into thy **mind** (<u>the heart, your understanding, the part of your body where you feel emotions</u>), and thou shalt **think** (<u>interlocked, weave, plot/contrive, regard, imagine, consider</u>) an evil **thought** (<u>a contrivance, an intention, plan, cunning work, curious work, imagination, invented, purpose</u>): 11 And thou shalt **say**, I will **go** up to the land of , . 12 **To take** (do) a spoil, and to take a prey; ,

In this chapter Ezekiel is directed to prophesy against the army of Gog. What we will be pulling out of this verse(s), is not the actual story or the message behind the story, but instead a process described in it. What God points out in the telling of this story is a process we go through called thinking.

This is a depiction of the way the process of thinking operates. It starts with "at the same time things come into your mind," step one. "You will think," step two. "An evil (or good) thought," step three. "And you will say or go or do," step four. One follows the other consistently time after time.

So let's take the first step of this process. Something comes to mind. This is the most important moment in the whole process. Although there are, what we can call, checkpoints throughout the process where we can turn back, the moment of decision to open the door or keep it closed to the thought will affect all other aspects of your day, potentially your life.

There are a myriad of ways that something comes to mind. People come to us with current information in conversation, we hear it on the news, we read it, we have memories from some time in the past that are triggered by sight and smell and music and conversation, and we have dreams and visions for the future.

When something comes to mind we feel something emotionally. Whether mild or strong, happy or sad, we have the choice to accept or decline or mull over the thought and corresponding emotion. We can preliminarily accept it for consideration, or outright decline it.

From my experience, the stronger the emotion whether pleasant or unpleasant corresponds with the level of difficulty involved in making the choice to open the door (or gate as mentioned yesterday) or keep the gate locked to a wicked potential intruder.

As we learned in yesterday's study, our minds process between 25,000 and 70,000 thoughts per day. Of those thoughts it is said that 70-80% are classified as negative. Is our gauge, as a Christ follower to be "positive or negative" or are we instructed to gauge as, "worldly or Godly"? They seem similar, just a different way to say the same thing…but that is not completely true. Positive gives the impression that it is a pleasant thought or action, and negative gives the impression that it is an unpleasant thought or action. This view of decision making is subjective, based on feelings and ideas, not necessarily in truth.

These worldly thoughts are based on feelings and experiential views. If we start at the beginning of this process and look at all things that come to mind through a veil of His precepts and principles, His truth, this is a Godly decision.

When you measure the virtue of allowing this to be considered and then accepted or declined based on Godly principles, not always is the plan and corresponding action to the thought process pleasant. But the outcome of making a Godly decision will be positive, even when unpleasant to carry out.

For example it doesn't feel good to restrain yourself from having a dessert at every meal, however the benefit of not doing so in both health benefits and how you feel when you step on the scales is worth the momentary discomfort in saying "no" to an oversized piece of your favorite cake.

Many times basing your decision on pleasant feelings or what seems to have a personal, business or social benefit, feels pleasant for a time until you get into it and things turn unpleasant. Why? The decision was not based on a God-based principle.

Based on this information, we are obliged to begin to operate differently than we may have in the past. Rather than opening the door to just any old thing that comes to mind, we need to be that gatekeeper we spoke of yesterday.

I just got a visual on this of a very wealthy person's home. We might consider it a mansion, but to him it is just home. He knows of his worth financially and to the community. He has not just a fence around his yard (what we might think of as a estate), but a strong wall with an iron gate.

This gate is not something that can be easily moved manually, but instead it is automated. Very few people would have a code to open this gate without first speaking to security. A person coming to visit casually or for business is screened. This screening process is first a virtual encounter. It is on a monitor and speaker.

If necessary and the person is important enough or if they are known to have an appointment the gatekeeper might come out in person. If that person is allowed past the gate, the owner of the property doesn't usually open the door of the mansion. No! One of the house staff, yet another layer of security, answers the door and more screening takes place before access to the owner is allowed. Then and only then is access received.

This is how we need to operate with the things that come to mind. Do we realize and protect our worth?

It takes focus. It takes diligence. This training season may take a long time, but is well worth the time and energy you put into it. The longer you practice this, the greater the benefit. As time goes by, you will see you as God sees you.

Good morning, Father. Thank you for heavenly protection and this aspect of screening that we are to take an active role in. In order for us to take full advantage of this we need to understand your desire for our lives. Please give us the desire to understand more and more. Each time we hear a teaching or read this word, we compound the wealth of knowledge you have promised us. Each time we open our heart to hearing a direction from the Holy Spirit, peace and favor and grace become magnified, not only for us to see, but that others will be blessed in the process by seeing our life. As thoughts come to mind we ask for a poke by the Holy Spirit so that we only allow fruitful things into our mind and thought process. Let peace be our guide in either allowing or denying access. Help us to stand firm when we are assailed by anything that does not align with your word. In Jesus' name, we praise and thank you, Amen!

Definitions for today's study:

Mind - from <H3823> (labab); **the heart** (as the most interior organ); used also like <H3820> (leb) :- + bethink themselves, **breast [your chest and heart, considered as the part of your body where you feel emotions]**, comfortably, courage, ([faint], [tender-] heart [-ed]), midst, mind, × unawares, **understanding**; a primitive root;

H3823 -properly to be enclosed (as if with fat); by implication (as denominative from <H3824> (lebab)) to unheart, i.e. (in a good sense) transport (with love), or (in a bad sense) stultify; also (as denominative from <H3834> (labiybah)) to make cakes :- make cakes, ravish, **be wise**.

H3820 - a form of <H3824> (lebab); the heart; also **used (figurative) very widely for the feelings**, the will and even the intellect; likewise for the centre of anything :- + care for, comfortably, consent, × considered, courag [-eous], friend [-ly], ([broken-], [hard-], [merry-], [stiff-], [stout-], double) heart ([-ed]), × heed, × I, kindly, midst, mind (-ed), × regard ([-ed]), × themselves, × unawares, **understanding**, × well, willingly, **wisdom**.

Think - a primitive root; properly **to plait or interpenetrate [penetrate mutually or be interlocked]**, i.e. (literal) **to weave** or (generally) to fabricate; figurative **to plot or contrive** (usually in a malicious sense); hence (from the mental effort) to think, **regard**, value, compute :- (make) account (of), **conceive**, **consider**, count, cunning (man, work, workman), devise, esteem, find out, forecast, hold, **imagine**, impute, invent, be like, mean, purpose, reckon (-ing be made), regard, think.

Thought - or machashebeth, makh-ash-eh"-beth; from <H2803> (chashab); **a contrivance**, i.e. (concrete) **a texture, machine, or (abstract) intention**, **plan (whether bad, a plot; or good, advice)** :- **cunning (work)**, **curious work**, device (-sed), **imagination**, **invented**, means, purpose, thought; *Primitive word is the same definition above for "think."*

CHAPTER 12

Beneficial Vital Principles

Ezekiel 38:10-12 (KJV)

10 Thus saith the Lord GOD; It shall also come to pass, that at the same time shall things come into thy **mind** (the heart, your understanding, the part of your body where you feel emotions), and thou shalt **think** (interlocked, weave, plot/contrive, regard, imagine, consider) an evil **thought** (a contrivance, an intention, plan, cunning work, curious work, imagination, invented, purpose): 11 And thou shalt **say**, I will **go** up to the land of , . 12 **To take** (do) a spoil, and to take a prey; ,

We are examining a process that we use thousands of times per day. This is a depiction of the way the process of thinking operates. It starts with "at the same time things come into your mind," step one. "You will think," step two. "An evil (or good) thought," step three. "And you will say or go or do," step four. One follows the other consistently time after time.

Yesterday we discussed the first step of the thinking process. Step one is the most important step, because it acts as the first gatekeeper to our mind. Changing our value used to gauge these thoughts that come to mind from positive or negative to worldly or Godly is key in this process. We have already described what a worldly thought is based on. Then what is Godly thought?

Godly things that come to mind are beneficial things. These are things that we find God has laid out for us in our owner's manual. They are instructional and will increase us, make us prosperous, and will nurture healing in our body, mind and heart. Let's look at that.

The only way we can understand the difference between what God says as beneficial versus those things that will prove harmful to us is through seeking first his kingdom. During this process of unlearning what took years to engrain in our mind and heart through wrong teachings from family, friends, educational systems, governmental systems and unfortunately some churches, we have the benefit of grace covering us and protecting us.

As our studies continue, we will see concepts within pages of the Bible that challenge almost everything we have learned previously. We will see the difference between what was common practice in our old life, against the standard of God's word.

It is normal to begin to ask questions of God. And we need to do this. God is not intimidated or angry when we do. He does not arrogantly tilt his head back, nose in the air and turn his back on us when we ask why it is better to do things this way or that. No, he encourages these questions.

1 John 4:1 Beloved, believe not every spirit, but try (test, approve, discern, examine, to think, to show) the spirits (soul, vital principle, mental disposition, mind), whether they are of God: because many false prophets (pretended

foreteller, plausible but false prophet) are gone out into the world.

When He tells us to test the spirits as in 1 John 4:1, He is telling us to examine or think about what is being said. Many times we need to step out in faith and follow the direction of the word before we see the results. However to ask about the wisdom behind his instruction is not wrong.

As a matter of fact the more we ask and gain that knowledge the easier it is to be an effective gatekeeper to our mind and heart. This process of talking to God about these things that come to mind is focused thinking. It is gatekeeping. It is admitting access to only the beneficial things and leaving the door shut on harmful things that come to mind.

Once preliminarily accepted we can consider with God the benefits or harmful effects of allowing the thought to stay with us. Sometimes wrestling takes place in this stage. It is not uncommon to allow access to something you have always allowed access to, only to find that you are impressed with some harmful aspect of this line of thought.

If it is decided that it is harmful you can put it out of your mind and close the gate. If it is decided that the thing is beneficial you can then continue thinking on it and discern its relevance in our life, begin to develop plans, solidify intentions and go into the action phase of the process, to say, to go and to do. This gatekeeping is key to seeing the plans and purposes of God play out in your life.

Good morning, Father. When I was first a member in this family of Christ, I thought I knew some things and at least the mask I wore in public indicated I knew a lot about life. I found out different as I began to go to church, study through reading the Bible, listening to tapes (CD's) and watching various teachers on the television. You have blessed me and others here with your gift of salvation, and your grace has not only saved us from problems that crop up in this life, but also opened our eyes to the truth or your word. We come in with a skewed understanding of who you are and what this life has to offer us, but your hand in our life straightens out that thinking. Thank you for helping us to see that this is not just about positive or negative thinking, but is about blocking the harmful thoughts and embracing the beneficial vital principles. You never meant for us to operate in our day to day dealings, as if we had a mask on and walking in a room we don't know, bumping around and getting hurt in the process. No! Our vision is to be clear, and when it is not we are to ask questions, dig in and camp out until the answers are revealed to us. Once we know the answer, we can no longer be tricked into harmful behavior, and are better equipped to help another. In Jesus' name, we praise and thank you, Amen!

Definitions for today's study:

Mind - from <H3823> (labab); **the heart** (as the most interior organ); used also like <H3820> (leb) :- + bethink themselves, **breast [your chest and heart, considered as the part of your body where you feel emotions]**, comfortably, courage, ([faint], [tender-] heart [-ed]), midst, mind, × unawares, **understanding**; a primitive root;

H3823 -properly to be enclosed (as if with fat); by implication (as denominative from <H3824> (lebab)) to unheart, i.e. (in a good sense) transport (with love), or (in a bad sense) stultify;

also (as denominative from <H3834> (labiybah)) to make cakes :- make cakes, ravish, **be wise**.

H3820 - a form of <H3824> (lebab); the heart; also **used (figurative) very widely for the feelings**, the will and even the intellect; likewise for the centre of anything :- + care for, comfortably, consent, × considered, courag [-eous], friend [-ly], ([broken-], [hard-], [merry-], [stiff-], [stout-], double) heart ([-ed]), × heed, × I, kindly, midst, mind (-ed), × regard ([-ed]), × themselves, × unawares, **understanding**, × well, willingly, **wisdom**.

Think - a primitive root; properly **to plait or interpenetrate [penetrate mutually or be interlocked]**, i.e. (literal) **to weave** or (generally) to fabricate; figurative **to plot or contrive** (usually in a malicious sense); hence (from the mental effort) to think, **regard**, value, compute :- (make) account (of), **conceive**, **consider**, count, cunning (man, work, workman), devise, esteem, find out, forecast, hold, **imagine**, impute, invent, be like, mean, purpose, reckon (-ing be made), regard, think.

Thought - or machashebeth, makh-ash-eh"-beth; from <H2803> (chashab); **a contrivance**, i.e. (concrete) **a texture, machine, or (abstract) intention**, **plan (whether bad, a plot; or good, advice)** :- **cunning (work)**, **curious work**, device (-sed), **imagination**, **invented**, means, purpose, thought; *Primitive word is the same definition above for "think."*

CHAPTER 13

Stable Thoughts, The Faith Connection

Romans 12:3 (KJV)

3 For I say, through the grace given unto me, to every man that is among you, not to think of himself more highly than he ought to think; but to think (exercise the mind) soberly (be of sound mind, in right mind, self-controlled, temperate or not given to extreme behavior or language), according (in that manner, in agreement with, because of the reason given) as God (the supreme Divinity, magistrate) hath dealt (distribute, divide, a division or share) to every man the measure (expressing a particular quantity) of faith (persuasion, moral conviction, reliance upon Christ, have confidence, increasingly confident).

I had not given a lot of thought to faith being connected with thinking until I came across this scripture in my search for the answer to why thinking is so necessary for us, and directed by God. But here it shows that connection.

The first part of the verse cautions us to bridle our thinking, to remain humble. "Don't think of yourself more highly than you ought." We are not to act as though we are better than other people. Now I think we need to measure this.

We can take this to a point of false humility by understating our skills and talents, by acting as though we are worms in the earth instead of a part of a royal family. This is not what is meant here. This is not saying that we have to hang around with every person who comes across our path, no matter their level of development or moral beliefs.

But instead, when gauging a person's actions to not condemn the person. It is not our role or within our authority or responsibility. However, it is necessary for us to bridle vanity.

We also need to be cognizant of our skills and talents. They have been given to us to by God to use for the benefit of mankind. To push them down and not give them place would be as arrogant as worshipping them. This is not indicating that we should not celebrate them, but worshipping them and making them higher than they should be is not appropriate. There will be some who misinterpret your confidence for arrogance or vanity. Keep this in mind.

The next portion of the verse discusses that we are to exercise our minds soundly, without extreme behavior or language. I see this in a person who responds in his time rather than to react emotionally to circumstances, someone who doesn't seem to waiver when a bad situation hits, and someone who isn't given to yelling or screaming but is calm under pressure. This person presents as solid. They walk in strength of character. Their mental process is calculated and reasonable.

If we are not that person today, we can be. We can begin to do this in agreement with the faith God has given us. We can begin to think with persuasion. We can begin to think soberly with moral conviction. We can begin to soberly exercise our mind with increasing confidence. Our self-controlled thinking can begin through reliance in Christ. We already have the appropriate measure of this faith to begin to be confident in our ability to think soundly.

Before we come into relationship with God, we do not understand how every principle and precept he has laid out for us to live a fruitful life are entwined with daily living. We don't need to wrap our minds around the vast amount of knowledge that is in the Bible before we can make progress in life. Gratefully we can and do build layers of understanding, improving day by day.

We start with understanding one precept, exercising our mind in that. Faith builds and increases. Thinking begins to travel into another area, new faith builds in this area. If we are starting at age 35-40, many ideas from years of unprofitable programming need to be undone. If we have been taught the precepts from an early age, our parents have put us in an elevated position. But no matter where we start, God's favor will advance us in ways we may have only dreamed of.

Good morning, Father. Thank you for helping us to see how faith and thinking are entwined. Faith is not an intangible concept without teeth; instead our strength builds the more we exercise this and our minds. Thank you for being that solid rock that our life is secured upon. Thank you for giving us faith that is so big that no matter where you take us in our thought process, we can be confident to develop ideas and concepts to their fullness. Thank you for stability that we have not had in the past, stability that will help our families, our friends and co-workers. Show us whom we can best help today. In Jesus' name, we praise and thank you, Amen!

Definitions for today's study:

Not - a primary particle of **qualified negation** (whereas <G3756> (ou) expresses an absolute denial); (adverb) not, (conjectire) lest; also (as interrogative implying a negative answer [whereas <G3756> (ou) expects an affirmative one]) whether :- any, but (that), × forbear, + God forbid, + lack, lest, neither, never, no (× wise in), none, nor, [can-] not, nothing, that not, un [-taken], without. Often used in compounds in substantially the same relations.

To think more - a primary preposition; properly near, i.e. (with general) from beside (literal or figurative), (with dative) at (or in) the vicinity of (object or subject), (with accusative) **to the proximity with (local [especially beyond or opposed to**] or causal [on account of]) :- above, against, among, at, before, by, contrary to, × friend, from, + give [such things as they], + that [she] had, × his, in, more than, nigh unto, (out) of, past, save, side ... by, in the sight of, than, [there-] fore, with. In compounds it retains the same variety of application.

Highly - from <G5228> (huper) and <G5426> (phroneo); **to esteem oneself overmuch**, i.e. **be vain or arrogant** :- think more highly. A COMBINATION OF a primary preposition; "over," i.e. (with the generic) of place, above, beyond, + from <G5424> (phren); **to exercise the mind**, i.e. entertain or have a sentiment or opinion; by implication to be (mentally) disposed (more or less earnestly in a certain direction); intensive to **interest oneself** in (with concern or obedience)

Ought - third person singular active present of <G1210> (deo); also deon, deh-on"; neuter active participle of the same; both used impersonal; it is (was, etc.) necessary (as binding) :- behoved, be meet, must (needs), (be) need (-ful), ought, should; a primary verb; to bind (in various applications, literal or figurative) :- bind, be in bonds, knit, tie, wind.

Think - from <G5424> (phren); **to exercise the mind**, i.e. **entertain or have a sentiment or opinion**; by implication to **be (mentally) disposed** (more or less earnestly in a certain direction); intensive to interest oneself in (with concern or obedience) :- set the affection on, (be) care (-ful), (be like-, + be of one, + be of the same, + let this) mind (-ed), regard, savour, think; probably from an obsolete phrao (to rein in or curb; compare <G5420> (phrasso)); the midrif (as a partition of the body), i.e. (figurative and by implication of sympathy) the feelings (or sensitive nature; by extension [also in the plural] the mind or cognitive faculties) :- understanding.
Soberly - from <G4998> (sophron); **to be of sound mind**, i.e. sane, (figurative) moderate :- **be in right mind**, be sober (minded), soberly; from the base of <G4982> (sozo) and that of <G5424> (phren); safe (sound) in mind, i.e. **self-controlled (moderate as to opinion or passion)** :- discreet, sober, **temperate [not extreme in behavior or language]** ; from a primary sos (contracted for obsolete saos, 'safe"); to save, i.e. deliver or protect (literal or figurative) :- heal, preserve, save (self), do well, be (make) whole + to reign in or curb.
According - probably adverb of comparative from <G3739> (hos); which how, i.e. **in that manner** (very variously used, as follows) :- about, after (that), (according) as (it had been, it were), as soon (as), even as (like), for, how (greatly), like (as, unto), since, so (that), that, to wit, unto, when ([-soever]), while, × with all speed.
Dealt - from <G3313> (meros); to part, i.e. (literal) to apportion, bestow, share, or (figurative) to disunite, differ :- deal, be difference between, distribute, divide, give participle; from an obsolete but more primary form of meiromai (to get as a section or allotment); **a division or share** (literal or figurative, in a wide application) :- behalf, coast, course, craft, particular (+ -ly), part (+ -ly), piece, portion, respect, side, some sort (-what).
Every man - as if a superlative of hekas (afar); each or every :- any, both, each (one), **every (man, one, woman)**, particularly.

Measure - an apparently primary word; **a measure** ("metre"), literal or figurative; by implication a limited portion (degree) :- measure.
Faith - from <G3982> (peitho); **persuasion**, i.e. credence; **moral conviction (of religious truth, or the truthfulness of God or a religious teacher)**, especially **reliance upon Christ** for salvation; abstract constancy in such profession; by extensive the system of religious (Gospel) **truth itself** :- assurance, belief, believe, faith, fidelity; a primary verb; **to convince (by argument, true or false)**; by analogy to pacify or conciliate (by other fair means); reflexive or passive to assent (to evidence or authority), **to rely (by inward certainty)** :- agree, assure, believe, **have confidence**, be **(wax) confident**, make friend, obey, persuade, trust, yield.

CHAPTER 14

Forgetting, Is It a Stretch? Get On With It!

Philippians 3:13 (KJV)

13 Brethren, I count not myself to have apprehended: but this one thing I do, forgetting (neglect, lie hidden, be ignorant, unawares) those things which are behind, and reaching forth unto (stretching, extend to) those things which are before (in front of),

This chapter is written by Paul. Early on the discussion covers a warning to be aware of contrary teachings and makes confession of his zealous past against followers of Christ. He states pretty clearly that he has not been perfected in his walk yet, but equates reaching the goal with the idea that he is forgetting the past (and his past behavior) and moving forward as key to his success.

Through our studies we have grown to understand that words (both the choice of and the placement of the word) are not a mistake in the Bible. We see here the word "forgetting," this indicates an ongoing process. Forgetting is to neglect a topic, superimposing a cover over something to keep it hidden, be ignorant of, or be unawares.

Now being able to forget on purpose is a concept that people who don't know God find very hard to do. I can only speak for myself, but there were things I had done in relationships, bad decisions in business that created failure, personal decisions that harmed my own heart in the past that I have had to set behind me or I would never have been able to move on.

Most of us have known someone in 12-step programs that have gone through all the steps including the "amends" step. There is a cleansing that takes place when asking to be forgiven by someone we have harmed and then taking that same step to forgive ourselves. People stay stuck in their obsession when they don't forgive and forget their past "offenses."

We have known business men/women who have acted with less than integrity in a weak moment, parents who would like to erase a screaming match with one of their kids, a husband or wife who have been unfaithful in finances, a friend who has not acted a friend, all of whom needed to go through a time of forgetting in order to move on to a more productive future.

People don't intentionally get themselves in trouble or desire to stay there once they are in the thick of it. And even when they are hooked by sin, there is an internal war that cartoons often played out by the little devil on one shoulder and the little angel on the other shoulder. They are engulfed in constant struggle, then once they find themselves in the family of Christ, they know their past and sometimes it is hard to receive this great gift of total forgiveness.

They may not realize that forgetting is every bit as important. If you don't do it, the past becomes a weight chained to your feet. It may not take you to the bottom of the ocean, but it certainly can keep you from thinking about a bright future. Get on with it, move forward.

This is how it worked for me. In the beginning, this felt a little like I was just skating though, getting an undeserved reprieve, so to speak. But isn't that grace?

It was not an easy process in part because I believed I needed to suffer for my offenses. I would tend to show mercy to another person, be gracious to them when they would apologize and often before they apologized. Yet, I would not give myself the same grace.

I had to remind myself that to hold on to my own sin (or anyone else's) was diluting the work that Jesus did in his death, burial and resurrection. When we don't forget and move on we place ourselves in the position of being our own god. Our decision not to forgive and forget errors from the past is in essence, saying that we know better than God how we should best be punished.

More people than you can imagine still hold onto the idea that both they and others have to pay for wrongs committed in the past. That is a wrong thought process, one we need to correct.

Learning that forgiving ourselves and then forgetting the past is part of the process God wants us to go through. I do have to say that if you neglect the ugliness of the past, ignore it and move on, the memory of it will still smart for a while. We spoke earlier of thoughts having emotion attached to them. A memory is a thought and so, when it pops back into your memory pain may accompany the memory for a while. I say for a while, because as time goes by and you have learned the lessons of those hard times, the pain of your offense lessens.

In the overall scheme of things, soon you will find that the memory looks more like an object lesson in a class or conference rather than an emotionally charged movie scene. It will become, as it was with Paul, something that he was able to use in his ministry or life work to help other people get past any place they may be stuck.

Good morning, Father. Thank you for showing us this aspect of thinking. Good morning, Father. Thank you for showing us this aspect of thinking. There will be times in our lives when amends are required for an offense. Once done we humbly apologize, we need to move into the "forgetting" mode. It is important for our healing and the healing of others in our circles. As a person who has gone through the healing process, we are placed in position to explain (selectively) our past to others with lessons attached in a move to help them through a similar tough time. We can hold a part of our life up as an object lesson to those coming behind us, in order that they not have to deal with similar pain. We can be used by you to assure others of your love and forgiveness by the words of our testimony. Thank you for helping us to assist another with our lessons learned today. In Jesus' name, we praise and thank you, Amen!

Definitions for today's study:

Forgetting - middle from <G1909> (epi) and <G2990> (lanthano); **to lose out of mind**; by implication **to neglect** :- (be) forget (-ful of); a primary preposition properly meaning superimposition (of time, place, order, etc.), as a relation of distribution [with the genitive], i.e. over, upon + a prolonged form of a primary verb, which is used only as an alternate in certain tenses; **to lie hid** (literal or figurative); often used adverb unwittingly :- be hid, **be ignorant of**, **unawares**.

Reaching forth unto - middle from <G1909> (epi) and <G1614> (ekteino); **to stretch (oneself) forward upon** :- reach forth; a primary preposition properly meaning superimposition (of time, place, order, etc.), as a relation of distribution [with the genitive], i.e. over, upon + from <G1537> (ek) and teino (to stretch); **to extend** :- cast, put forth, stretch forth (out); or ex, ex; a primary preposition denoting origin

Before - from <G1722> (en) and <G4314> (pros); **in front of** (in place [literal or figurative] or time) :- against, at, before, (in presence, sight) of.

CHAPTER 15

Umpires and Referees

Hebrews 6:12 (KJV)

12 That ye be not slothful (sluggish, lazy, stupid, dull), but followers of them who through faith (persuasion, moral conviction, be or increase in confidence) and patience (good-natured tolerance, ability to be polite, calm and patient in hard times, strength of mind enabling to endure) inherit the promises.

This verse holds up our predecessor in faith, Abraham, as an example for our future thoughts and beliefs, speech and actions. This verse picks it up on one of the threads of thought in this book, and that is that making any profitable change in our lives requires our participation and dedication. It is saying our predecessors were not slothful, and we need to follow their lead.

Prior to looking at the definition, my understanding was that being slothful was strictly a physical lack of action or physical laziness. And although that is true, it is not a full description. This definition shows us that slothfulness can occur in our thinking and believing as well. We grow mentally or emotionally or spiritually lazy the same way we grow physically lazy.

Stop to think of that teenage athlete who works out daily for the years he is in middle school and carries that on to his early athletic “career” in his high school years. This guy has a goal in mind. It could be that he wants the status of being in the spotlight. It could be that he simply loves the sport. It could be that he sees a talent that will help him scholarship into college.

Whatever the foundational reason for playing sports, in order to perform well and remain playing he is required to keep his body fit. Once he has gotten that scholarship and goes into the freshman year in college he keeps working out and playing to keep the scholarships in place. This activity continues until he either quits sports or completes school and moves into life outside of college.

Once he has graduated and moves into the nine to five work world he finds that his job requires so many hours that several days a week he just can’t make it to the gym. In college, his job was working out and studying. Now his job is working to care for his family, functioning in everyday life. He doesn’t notice much of a change immediately. However, little by little internal changes toward deterioration are taking place under the surface.

After several years, he begins to notice that his metabolism has geared down significantly, that he has gotten lazy in this area out of a shift of priorities. It doesn’t take too many years for his body to lose muscle tone. Lowered metabolism and lack of daily exercises have cycled into a flabby physique and extra pounds.

The same thing happens with our thinking. We have spoken about the link between thinking and believing. Each new thought piles up and begins to build a little city of different thoughts or beliefs. Thinking builds both intellectual and spiritual muscles, so to speak.

Thinking contributes more than most understand to the emotional muscles we have, too. The youth spoken about in the story above disciplined his body throughout several years to gain the physical attributes needed to qualify and excel in his sport. I'm sure that there were times when it would have been so much more pleasurable to sleep in late rather than get to his work out, but he made a daily choice to flex his muscles.

As we go from childhood into adulthood, our life gets off balance by the responsibility load we carry. As time goes by we might have an idea that we have let our thinking (knowledge gathering and separation and storage) slip.

Without realizing it we have allowed others to think for us in several areas of life. They have presented themselves as experts, and of course they know better than we do, right? In many cases, we have allowed religious leaders, politicians, media and medical experts (the great they) make decisions for us. We didn't take the time to research these decisions and hold them up to God's standard, but accepted them at face value. It didn't happen all at once but instead, little by little.

Our society as a whole has become lazy. People are unaware of their piece in the life puzzle. They do not know how valuable their beliefs are to society and that their voice matters. They may not have been validated much of their lives. When this happens you have groups people who believe what the universal "they," the authoritative "they" say is possible or impossible in their lives.

We have a society that has taken the Bible and biblical principles out of everything from educational systems, to government, to entertainment. Each of these systems that originally were set up to be useful for the populous are now steering the thought process farther away from the Maker and the owner's manual he has given us.

We have been told that these things are no longer relevant. And yet, those of us who begin to use the principles, even for the first time begin to get results that are spelled out in the book.

Instead of having no muscles in many areas of our spiritual, emotional and intellectual life, we can begin making positive changes by using the word of God as our guide to evaluate information that comes to us. Contrary to popular talking points, it remains relevant in today's world.

Naysayers, those with aggressively negative views regarding Godly principles will be noisy when we begin to think about things and stand up for Biblical principles. That's okay! It feels good to exercise the mind. And as these muscles build we will find that confusion leaves.

Confusion just doesn't have legs once we bring some basic absolutes into the picture. We no longer end up being the athlete running from one end of the field to the other waiting for the umpire/referee make a call on a play. We become the referee/umpire. He knows the sport inside and out. He needs to keep up physically to keep his eyes on plays, he needs critical thinking skills, quick thinking, common sense and confidence in knowing the guidelines. Our new sport is to umpire information with the Bible as our rulebook and God as our sports commissioner.

Good morning, Father. Thank you for helping us to see that we are not here only to play the sport of life, but to be the administrator of the game. You have given us the privilege of becoming involved on the field, but only with exercising one of our most valued muscles (the one between our ears) will we have the means to move on this directive. We know that thinking is a spiritual function, and you speak to us through our mind and heart. We ask for favor in this, especially in a day and time when so much of our lives seem to be controlled by people who are simply not aware of your ways. We ask for your help to be more alert in all we do. In Jesus' name, we praise and thank you, Amen!

Definitions for today's study:

Slothful - from a derivative of <G3541> (nothos); **sluggish**, i.e. (literal) **lazy**, or (figurative) **stupid** :- **dull**, slothful; of uncertain affinity; a spurious or illegitimate son :- bastard.

Followers - from <G3401> (mimeomai); **an imitator** :- follower; middle from mimos (a "**mimic**"); to imitate :- follow.

Faith - from <G3982> (peitho); **persuasion**, i.e. credence; **moral conviction** (of religious truth, or the truthfulness of God or a religious teacher), especially reliance upon Christ for salvation; abstract constancy in such profession; by extensive the system of religious (Gospel) truth itself :- assurance, belief, believe, faith, fidelity; a primary verb; to convince (by argument, true or false); by analogy to pacify or conciliate (by other fair means); reflexive or passive to assent (to evidence or authority), to rely (by inward certainty) :- agree, assure, believe, have confidence, **be (wax) confident**, make friend, obey, persuade, trust, yield.

Patience - from the same as <G3116> (makrothumos); **longanimity [good-natured tolerance of delay]**, i.e. (objective) **forbearance [the ability to be polite, calm, and patient]** or (subjective) **fortitude [strength of mind that enables one to**

endure adversity with courage] :- longsuffering, patience; adverb of a compound of <G3117> (makros) and <G2372> (thumos); with long (enduring) temper, i.e. leniently :- patiently; combination of lengthy + from <G2380> (thuo); passion (as if breathing hard) :- fierceness, indignation, wrath. Compare <G5590> (psuche).

Inherit - from <G2818> (kleronomos); to be an heir to (literal or figurative) :- be heir, (obtain by) inherit (-ance); from <G2819> (kleros) and the base of <G3551> (nomos) (in its original sense of partitioning, i.e. [reflexive] getting by apportionment); a sharer by lot, i.e. an inheritor (literal or figurative); by implication a possessor :- heir; combination of portion, heritage, inheritance, lot + parcel out.

Promises - from <G1861> (epaggello); an announcement (for information, assent or pledge; especially a divine assurance of good) :- message, **promise [give grounds for expectations]**; from <G1909> (epi) and the base of <G32> (aggelos); to announce upon (reflexive), i.e. (by implication) **to engage to do something**, to assert something respecting oneself :- profess, (make) promise;

CHAPTER 16

From Obscurity into the Light

1 Peter 5:8 (KJV)

8 Be sober (discreet, abstain from wine, watch, approach with a serious attitude), be vigilant (to keep awake, idea of collecting one's faculties, rouse from sleep); because your adversary (an opponent, the opposite of right and justice) the devil (a traducer, false accuser, slanderer), as a roaring lion, walketh about, seeking whom he may devour (to drink down, swallow up):

A sober and vigilant attitude will take you places you may have only dreamed of and will help you keep that ground gained (and rise to higher levels if you choose) once there.

Acting sober is the opposite of the way a person acts when they have drunk too much alcohol. A "drunk" person is unable to control their speech and actions, even their behavior. If you have seen someone in this state their ability to think rationally is impaired, decision making at a time when you are drunk could be disastrous. Inhibitions are reduced sometimes to almost nothing. People do and say things in this state that could just be humorous to the onlooker, but can also be embarrassing come the light of day.

I know there are decisions that I have made in my past that appeared as though I must have been drinking in order to come up with any "logical" reason to have decided in this manner. It would have been easier to say that I was drunk when the decision was made, than to own the fact that I had not used discretion. It is hard to admit I was not being focused in my thought process, nor did I look at the situation with a serious attitude, one that took my future into account (whether physical, financial or emotional).

During a time like this you are not weighing the consequences, or how this will affect you or your family. You may be looking at a financial decision that if not considered thoughtfully could create a deficit for which you (and your family) might regret for decades to come. You may be considering a second marriage. What you decide could be the difference between harmony and well-adjusted children or heartache for all involved. You may be silently eating or drinking yourself into ill-health, not realizing how certain foods can benefit or destroy the cells.

Vigilance is similar to part of yesterday's topic about coming to our senses regarding some of the decisions we allowed the "great they" make for us in politics and government, education, and religion. It holds in it the idea of rousing yourself out of a sleep or inactivity, or even from obscurity. Why obscurity?

Well, obscurity is like hiding. Hiding is often caused by the fear of taking responsibility and facing change. Lackadaisical attitudes toward our responsibility for our thoughts, decisions and actions, allow us the means to hide. When we choose to be vigilant in our thought life, it is like turning on the light in a room. All of a sudden we see our responsibility in circumstances in a new light.

By no longer hiding from a set of circumstances, fears or people and deciding to face them head on, you are eliminating the effect that circumstance can have on you. Isn't it one of the enemy's greatest tools against us? Fear generated by threats to our family, our health, our finances, .fear of what will happen if you do (fill in the blank), or fear of what will happen if you don't (fill in the blank).

But when you wake up, collect your faculties and make the decision to stay awake, things will be changed for the better in your life. You can still have fun, cut up, joke and laugh while being fully awake, fully serious about your life and the decision you face.

Good morning, Father. Thank you for showing us that it is more possible to live in joy and happiness when we have serious attitudes on foundational issues of life. Thank you for waking us up to one or more areas of our life that we need to face an issue before it gets the better of us. When an issue gets the better of us what is left over is not the best, we are left with fragments and usually not very good ones to piece together. But knowing you, Father, is our strong suit. You can and will make us whole in areas where we have been fragmented. Give us strength to face what needs to be faced, and once we have gained ground there help us to do whatever necessary to maintain it. We love you Lord and ask for an opportunity to serve someone today. In Jesus' name, we praise and thank you, Amen!

Definitions used in today's study:
Sober - of uncertain affinity; to abstain from wine (keep sober), i.e. (figurative) **be discreet [marked by prudence or modesty and wise self-restraint, heedful of potential consequences,**

PRUDENT; WISE IN AVOIDING ERRORS OR EVIL, AND IN SELECTING THE BEST MEANS TO ACCOMPLISH A PURPOSE; CIRCUMSPECT; CAUTIOUS; WARY; NOT RASH.] :- be sober, **watch [forbearance of sleep]** . Dictionary definition of sober: with serious attitude. Dictionary definition of attitude: a complex mental state involving beliefs and feelings and values and dispositions to act in certain ways.

Vigilant - from <G1453> (egeiro); **to keep awake**, i.e. watch (literal or figurative) :- be vigilant, wake, (be) watch (-ful); probably akin to the base of <G58> (agora) (**through the idea of collecting one's faculties**); to waken (transitive or intransitive), i.e. **rouse (literal from sleep, from sitting or lying, from disease, from death; or figurative from obscurity, inactivity, ruins, nonexistence)** :- awake, lift (up), **raise (again, up)**, rear up, (a-) rise (again, up), stand, take up

Adversary - from <G473> (anti) and <G1349> (dike); **an opponent** (in a lawsuit); specially Satan (as the arch-enemy) :- adversary; combination of a primary particle; **opposite**, i.e. instead or because of (rarely in addition to) :- for, in the room of. Often used in composition to denote contrast, requital, substitution, correspondence, etc + probably from <G1166> (deiknuo); **right (as self-evident)**, i.e. **justice (the principle, a decision**, or its execution) :- judgment, punish, vengeance; a prolonged form of an obstract primary of the same meaning; to show (literal or figurative) :- shew.

Devil - from <G1225> (diaballo); **a traducer [one who attacks the reputation of another by slander or libel]**; specially Satan [compare <H7854> (satan)] :- **false accuser**, devil, s**landerer**; from <G1223> (dia) and <G906> (ballo); (figurative) to **traduce [to say things that will harm someone's reputation, speak unfavorably about]** :- accuse; combination of a primary preposition denoting **the channel of an act**; through (in very wide applications, local, causal or occasional) :- after, always, among, at, to avoid, because of (that), briefly, by, for (cause)...fore, from, in, by occasion of, of, by reason of, for sake, that, thereby, therefore, × though, through (-out), to, wherefore, with (-in). In composition it retains the same general

import + a primary verb; **to throw (in various applications, more or less violent or intense)** :- arise, cast (out), × dung, lay, lie, pour, put (up), send, strike, throw (down), thrust. Compare <G4496> (rhipto);
the word satan (G7854) - from <H7853> (satan); **an opponent**; especially (with the article prefixed) Satan, **the arch-enemy of good** :- **adversary**, Satan, withstand; a primitive root; **to attack**, (figurative) **accuse** :- (be an) adversary, resist.
As – which how; **in that manner**
Devour - from <G2596> (kata) and <G4095> (pino); **to drink down**, i.e. **gulp entire** (literal or figurative) :- devour, drown, **swallow (up)**; a primary particle; (preposition) down (in place or time), in varied relations (according to the case [general, dative or accusative] with which it is joined) :- about, according as (to), after, against, (when they were) × alone, among, and, × apart, (even, like) as (concerning, pertaining to, touching), × aside, at, before, beyond, by, to the charge of, [charita-] bly, concerning, + frequently denotes opposition, distribution or intensity + a prolonged form of pio, pee"-o, which (together with another form poo, po"-o) occurs only as an alternate in certain tenses; to imbibe (literal or figurative) :- drink.

CHAPTER 17

Powerless Without Cooperation

1 Peter 5:8 (KJV)

8 Be sober, be vigilant; because your adversary the devil, as a roaring lion, walketh about, seeking whom he may devour:

Okay, I have to begin this by telling on myself. I couldn't help but laugh. This shows that God can take any mistake and turn it around. As usual when I began laying this study out I pulled up the definitions for key words from Strong's Concordance and added to the reference area at the end of the email/blog. Then I read over the words within the definition to see if there are certain words that either hit a particular chord with me or those that I need to clarify definition through the use of a dictionary (which I add to the definition before writing the study paragraphs).

Keep in mind that over the last couple of weeks we have been targeting our thought process, why it is important and how widely our perceptions and beliefs affect our faith and everyday life.

Looking at the first word to define "devil" I saw (or should I say perceived) this word as transducer (if you glance below, it is really traducer). So I pulled up the definition of transducer which is "a piece of equipment that gets power from one source and then changes that power so that it can be used by another system."

Immediately my mind began to develop a visual on this. But I continued looking at the other words within the definition. I then saw "the channel of an act" like "through," which seemed to support the word transducer. Then the next very relevant word "traduce" shows up in the list. Lo and behold, it hit me! The word I had read as "transducer" was "traduce." Did I ever have a laugh!

I couldn't get over the thought process that had begun to take place when I read the definition of transducer and how it seemed to fit well with "a channel of acts." We can't discount the fact that the devil is a channel of acts. We can't discount the fact that he attempts to get us to use our power and strength for his work rather than kingdom work. He attempts to sway the mind and heart of people to disbelieve God's principles and through his act of traducing, convincing them he is able to carry out his mission of destruction. So let's look at this.

The thing is the definition of transducer coincides with "the channel of an act."

- Transducer: a piece of equipment that gets power from one source and then changes that power so that it can be used by another system

- A channel: a method of sending or receiving, like communicating information; or use energy, ability or ideas for a particular purpose; to send something along a passage

As an example the loud speaker is a transducer in that it takes electrical impulses and changes it to sound. It takes electrical impulses or power going into one end (of the channel, so to speak) and changes that power (or impulse) to be used by our ears as sound. I don't see that this is much different from what goes on with the devil.

He has been divested of any real power. He has no body, he has no audible voice, and is powerless without our cooperation. He comes to us, knocking on the door of our mind with lies and accusations. If we allow him access he is able through our power to use our thought process, our speech and our actions. This verse says he comes like a roaring lion not that he is one. Do we want to be a transducer by which he can operate? Do we want him to use our power and with our help change that power so it can be used by his system rather than God's system (kingdom)?

Good morning, Father. Thank you for helping me to turn this mistake in perception to something usable by us all. You have given us power that we are to use to accomplish our tasks day to day, our purpose in life, to carry out benevolent acts in your behalf. Help us to understand that when we believe the lies of the devil (a traducer) and speak or act contrary to your principles, we are basically allowing our strength to be polluted and used by the wrong system. We choose to soberly stand guard at the gate of our mind, allowing access to all that is good and useful. We open ourselves to serve someone who needs our assistance today. In Jesus' name, we praise and thank you, Amen!

Definitions used in today's study:

Devil - from <G1225> (diaballo); **a traducer [one who attacks the reputation of another by slander or libel]**; specially Satan

[compare <H7854> (satan)] :- **false accuser**, devil, s**landerer**; from <G1223> (dia) and <G906> (ballo); (figurative) to **traduce [to say things that will harm someone's reputation, speak unfavorably about]** :- accuse; combination of a primary preposition denoting **the channel of an act**; through (in very wide applications, local, causal or occasional) :- after, always, among, at, to avoid, because of (that), briefly, by, for (cause)...fore, from, in, by occasion of, of, by reason of, for sake, that, thereby, therefore, × though, through (-out), to, wherefore, with (-in). In composition it retains the same general import + a primary verb; **to throw (in various applications, more or less violent or intense)** :- arise, cast (out), × dung, lay, lie, pour, put (up), send, strike, throw (down), thrust. Compare <G4496> (rhipto);
the word satan (G7854) - from <H7853> (satan); **an opponent**; especially (with the article prefixed) Satan, **the arch-enemy of good** :- **adversary**, Satan, withstand; a primitive root; **to attack**, (figurative) **accuse** :- (be an) adversary, resist.
As – which how; **in that manner**
Devour - from <G2596> (kata) and <G4095> (pino); **to drink down**, i.e. **gulp entire** (literal or figurative) :- devour, drown, **swallow (up)**; a primary particle; (preposition) down (in place or time), in varied relations (according to the case [general, dative or accusative] with which it is joined) :- about, according as (to), after, against, (when they were) × alone, among, and, × apart, (even, like) as (concerning, pertaining to, touching), × aside, at, before, beyond, by, to the charge of, [charita-] bly, concerning, + frequently denotes opposition, distribution or intensity + a prolonged form of pio, pee"-o, which (together with another form poo, po"-o) occurs only as an alternate in certain tenses; to imbibe (literal or figurative) :- drink.

CHAPTER 18

Distorted Truths, the Downfall of Rulers

Ephesians 4:23 (KJV)

23 And be renewed (renovated, reformed – change that is intended to correct a situation) in the spirit (mental disposition – a tendency to behave in a certain way, the Spirit of God) of your mind (the intellect, understanding, be sure);

In Ephesians 4:22 is a warning telling us to put off our former conversation. The first description in the definition of the word translated "conversation" is behavior, and the root word means to overturn, or return. The word overturn means to say officially that something such as a decision or law is wrong and then change it, or cause the downfall of rulers.

These words clearly indicate that before we came to know Jesus there was another "ruler" directing our steps, that we were governed by other thoughts or laws. It is not a stretch to say that both our conversation and outward behavior reflected this. That old man was spoiled by a delusion that living in lustful thinking was the way to go. Lustful thinking is not only in the sexual realm. We can have lust in other areas of life as well.

Ephesians 4:23 picks up by telling us how, by the renewal of the spirit of our mind putting off former conversation occurs. This happens immediately in our spirit man upon asking and receiving Jesus as Lord and Savior. We can see some miraculous changes in folk's behavior manifesting nearly immediately when they make this life changing choice.

An example of this, for me, was that almost immediately I had a change in my speech. For years my speech was peppered with cuss words. I mean some pretty foul language. I would be lying if I told you that I ever tried to curtail this speech. The rough edge on me seemed to serve me well (at least in my mind's eye). I was competing in a man's world in business and could cuss with the best/worst of them. But from the time that I accepted Jesus as Lord, I stopped swearing. The desire to speak using cuss words fled from me. I no longer even wanted to cuss and I began to use my vocabulary to express myself as clearly without the shock value added. It was an amazing outward sign. I could say "God did this!"

These types of changes in the spirit of our mind occur sometimes without our active participation as in my story. But then there are other changes that occur with our active participation with study, prayer and meditation, the active pursuit of truth. Most of my personal changes have taken much longer than the instantaneous change of speech at conversion, and have only happened as I became fully convinced and I understood deeper truths.

Learning new thought processes requires repetition. We don't typically believe a truth as soon as we hear or see it. There will more often than not be something inside that agrees with the truth filled precept or principle. That something is the Holy Spirit who is confirming the word in our understanding. Our accepting the truth can take some convincing.

However if we have been living a distorted truth that fits our current way of life, our flesh will try to talk us out of God's principle as outlined in the word. During the repetition phase (rehearing the word in different verses, in teachings by our pastors or evangelists) we can and should be questioning God. "Is this so?" or "Why?" or "How do I change this?"

Again, God is not upset or confused that we question. He has told us to "test the spirits." If we don't first question his spirit, wrestling with these new precepts in our spirit and getting our answers, how will we be able to wrestle effectively with deceitful spirits and know the difference between their voice and His?

This repetition brings intensity or strength in the new line of thought and our faith to stand on it. New and focused thought based in God's truth brings new speech and outward behavior or actions. Our mind is a spiritual tool in our life. We need to use it well.

Good morning, Father. Thank you for immediate changes that we see when you lay your hand on us. We are so grateful for this. Thank you for those changes that can only occur when your Holy Spirit works with us in digging out understanding through study. We are so grateful for this most powerful spiritual tool called the mind. With your help we are learning to be focused and diligent in our thoughts, through this directed action we will see great moves of the Holy Spirit to change those things in us that have troubled us for years. With these changes, we will be better equipped to serve others you bring across our path. In Jesus' name, we praise and thank you, Amen!

Definition used in today's study:

Renewed - from <G303> (ana) and a derivative of <G3501> (neos); **to renovate**, i.e. **reform [a change that is intended to correct a situation]** :- renew; a primary preposition and adverb; properly up; but (by extension) used (distributively) severally, or (locally) at (etc.) :- and, apiece, by, each, every (man), in, through. **In compounds (as a prefix) it often means (by implication) repetition, intensity, reversal, etc.**

Spirit - from <G4154> (pneo); a current of air, i.e. breath (blast) or a breeze; by analogy or figurative a spirit, i.e. (human) the rational soul, (by implicaiton) vital principle, **mental disposition [tendency to behave in a certain way],** etc., or (superhuman) an angel, dæmon, or **(divine) God**, **Christ's spirit**, **the Holy Spirit** :- ghost, life, spirit (-ual, -ually), mind. Compare <G5590> (psuche).

Mind - probably from the base of <G1097> (ginosko); **the intellect**, i.e. mind (**divine or human; in thought, feeling, or will**); by implication meaning :- mind, understanding. Compare <G5590> (psuche); a prolonged form of a primary verb; to "know" (absolute), in a great variety of applications and with many implication (as follow, with others not thus clearly expressed) :- allow, be aware (of), feel, (have) know (-ledge), perceive, be resolved, can speak, be sure, understand.

CHAPTER 19

Determined Consideration & Wisdom

Ecclesiastes 9:1 (KJV)

1 For all this I considered (admit openly, make no bones about it; discover by examining evidence, determine with certainty) in my heart (feelings, will, intellect, understanding, wisdom) even to declare all this, that the righteous, and the wise, and their works, are in the hand of God: no man knoweth either love or hatred by all that is before them.

The first word in this study is one of my favorites that we have studied in the past. This is the word that is used whenever we see "Thus saith the Lord." As we pointed out in earlier studies this word is a definite declaration that something is. It means to avouch.

Avouch is to admit openly and bluntly, it is to make no bones about it. It means to declare or assert with positiveness, to maintain, vindicate, or justify; to make good; answer for; establish; guarantee; substantiate, evidence; testimony; and/or an assurance.

Its root is vouch which denotes a personal guarantee. A voucher is not only someone who gives the guarantee, but also an official piece of paper that you can use instead of money to buy a particular product or service. You can take it to the bank. It is sure.

It is the word translated 'saith" or in this case "consider." This is not just a word of declaration, but one that means that the declaration is based on focused thought. People say a lot of things that don't have substance to them. But when we read the first part of this verse we see clearly that the thought behind this declaration has a basis (foundation, grounds) to it.

This declaration was determined by examining evidence, by taking time and making an effort to inquire about the subject before speaking. This declaration is made only after careful consideration. The opinion stated was mulled over and the truth of it was searched out before the author spoke it.

This is how we are to be living our lives. When we do take time to examine the evidence before we answer a question, a statement, an offer, or an accusation, we will with God's assistance get to the truth of a matter.

We live in a time when communication happens quickly. People imply that they require an immediate response to the words and actions played out in the theatre of our day. But we have control. There is no need to respond immediately to most words or actions that knock at our doors.

If we have taken time and studied a subject or an aspect of life and have developed an informed stance, our response can be quicker than if we are ignorant in a subject. When we do not know, we need to examine before we open our mouths. Even when we do know and have a stance, we still have control over when we choose to respond or if we will (or will not) respond.

Just because someone is saying something, doesn't mean that we have an obligation to answer. The more sure we are of God and our stand in life, the less often we feel an obligation to crumble under someone's attempt to apply pressure to us in order to initiate an answer. It is always prudent to take the time to speak with God about the wisdom of answering any communication. Sometimes it serves us better to remain silent.

Good morning, Father. Thank you for increasing maturity, for an understanding that the more we know, the more there is to know. Knowledge, understanding and wisdom come in layers. These things are not poured on us as an avalanche that will bury us and make us ineffective. No! Layers upon layers of information brought to us by you. Some things we don't understand why we need until years later when we are in the thick of a conversation or project where these pearls of wisdom are there for our use. There is no greater source of information, understanding of that information and the wisdom to use it properly than You, our God. Guide us in our search for truth. Bring to us the people, circumstances and information needed to properly navigate the world. Show us those pieces of information brought to us for the benefit of others, and give us eyes to see where we can serve with this wisdom. In Jesus' name, we praise and thank you, Amen!

Definitions used in today's study:

Considered - a primitive root; **to say** (used with great latitude) :- **answer**, **appoint**, **avouch**, bid, boast self, call, certify, challenge, charge, + (at the, give) command (-ment), commune, consider, declare, demand, × desire, **determine**, × expressly, × indeed, × intend, name, × plainly, promise, publish, report, require, say, speak (against, of), × still, × suppose, talk, tell, term, × that is, × think, use [speech], utter, × verily, × yet.

Heart - a form of <H3824> (lebab); the heart; also used (figurative) very widely for **the feelings, the will and even the intellect**; likewise for **the centre of anything** :- + care for, **comfortably**, **consent**, × **considered**, courag [-eous], friend [-ly], ([broken-], [hard-], [merry-], [stiff-], [stout-], double) heart ([-ed]), × heed, × I, kindly, midst, **mind** (-ed), × **regard** ([-ed]), × themselves, × unawares, **understanding**, × well, willingly, **wisdom**; from <H3823> (labab); the heart (as the most interior organ); used also like <H3820> (leb) :- + **bethink themselves**, breast, comfortably, **courage**, ([faint], [tender-] heart [-ed]), midst, **mind**, × unawares, understanding; a primitive root; properly to be enclosed (as if with fat); by implication (as denominative from <H3824> (lebab)) to unheart, i.e. (in a good sense) transport (with love), or (in a bad sense) stultify; also (as denominative from <H3834> (labiybah)) to make cakes :- make cakes, ravish, **be wise**.

Declare - a primitive root; to bore, i.e. (figurative) examine :- declare.

CHAPTER 20

Government Exemption, Blessed Assurance

Ecclesiastes 9:1 (KJV)

1 For all this I considered (admit openly, make no bones about it; discover by examining evidence, determine with certainty) in my heart (feelings, will, intellect, understanding, wisdom) even to declare all this, that the righteous (just, lawful, cleanse, make wise [in mind, word, or act]), and the wise (intelligent, skillful or artful; cunning, subtil, make wiser), and their works (a deed, service), are in the hand (the open one, indicating power, means and direction) of God: no man knoweth (ascertain by seeing, recognition, instruction, comprehend, be learned) either love or hatred by all that is before them.

Yesterday we spoke about not living our lives continually shooting from the hip. Or could we say, shooting from the lip?

We spoke of the importance of considering issues, accusations and information that comes to us carefully before declaring our stand. It is not always necessary or prudent to make our thoughts known and when we choose to make our declarations timing is important. We have a right and even responsibility to do this in our (and God's) timing.

This verse and so many others point to the idea that God's timing, will and heart are in a continuing melding process with our own heart and mind the more entwined our relationship becomes. As the requestor, we seldom have the right to demand the timing of our answer.

Stop and think of the times someone has attempted to pressure you into a business deal, signing a contract for a car loan, a handsome suitor or pretty damsel pressuring for more in a relationship. Pressure is a tactic used by Satan to make us think that there are time limits that can't be overridden. Pressure is meant to divert us from a Godly path.

Oh, and by the way God is God. He is not accustomed to succumbing to outside pressure. If this is the case for Him, and we were made in His image, are we to succumb?

The second part of this verse says that the righteous and the wise are in the hands of God. The righteous spoken of is us, born-again men and women of God. The wise, intelligent, skillful, cunning, and subtle spoken of here is us. It says that all of our daily deeds and service to others are in the hand of God.

He gives us our righteousness, and the desire to do righteous acts. It is through wrestling mentally and spiritually that we come to have His mind and wisdom dwelling in us. That wisdom needs to be accessed through our thought process.

Every time we are faced with a decision and decide to choose wisdom over foolishness it is a mind/heart activity. As we submit to His direction, we tend to act godlier. We choose to serve where we may have held back in the past. We give financially in greater amounts, because we see needs in a keener light. We also know He not only has the means but has promised to multiply our giving (Jesus discussed in the parable of seed time and harvest). Our wisdom grows as we spend more time in our relationship with Him. It is then up to us to apply the principles and lessons learned to our daily living.

The last portion of the verse and the beginning of the next verse of this chapter tell us that we all experience the same kind of problems, whether we are considered righteous or not. We all run into the same kind of circumstances. We all have positive and negative thoughts come knocking at the door of our minds. We all experience happy or sad life events, regardless of our spiritual stand.

Life happens to the righteous and unrighteous people alike. It tells us that whether we are givers or not, whether we are wrong or right, basically "as is the good so is the sinner". The same events occur to all, and also we all have the ability to consider and then respond to these in either a righteous or unrighteous manner.

Life is not just a bowl of cherries because we have come into the kingdom. Our act of receiving Jesus as Lord doesn't exempt us from trouble coming to knock on our door. Before we come into the family, we are subject to worldly laws and principle. Added to this most "good" folks also attempt, at least in part, to live up to the more Godly precepts of universal good (i.e. the Ten

Commandments, do unto others as you would have them do to you, etc.).

However, once in the family we become subject to God's precepts and principles and we have an exemption to the worldly way of doing things. Exempt means - allowed to ignore something such as a rule, obligation, or payment; grant relief or an exemption from a rule or requirement; (of persons) freed from or not subject to an obligation or liability (as e.g. taxes) to which others or other things are subject. So we have a choice, an avenue of escape so to speak.

When we know the precepts, when we know how the principles work, then we can choose a Godly response over a worldly reaction. This is where we benefit from our studies, and speaking God's word over our lives.

Good morning, Father. Thank you for making it clear that all of us face the same kinds of life events as our neighbor. Life events happen whether we are in the family or not. Thank you for ready access to your guidance, wisdom and supply, and that we can access this fullness and respond responsibly to all matters we face. Our prayer today is that we provide testimony through our day to day activities and responses to others. Help us be an appropriate ambassador and that others will be able to see You through us. We thank you for an extraordinary favor as we go out in our activities today. Please show us that person/organization that you desire us to be involved in serving. In Jesus' name, we praise and thank you, Amen!

Definitions used in today's study:

Righteous - from <H6663> (tsadaq); just :- **just**, **lawful**, **righteous** (man); a primitive root; to be (causative make) right (in a moral or forensic sense) :- cleanse, clear self, (be, do) just (-ice, -ify, -ify self), (be, turn to) righteous (-ness).

Wise - from <H2449> (chakam); wise, (i.e. **intelligent, skilful or artful**) :- **cunning** (man), **subtil [Nice; fine; delicate]**, ([un-]), wise ([hearted], man); a primitive root, to be wise (in mind, word or act) :- × exceeding, **teach wisdom**, be (make self, shew self) wise, deal (never so) wisely, **make wiser**.

Works - from <H5647> (`abad); **a deed** :- work; a primitive root; to work (in any sense); by implication **to serve**, till, (causative) enslave, etc. :- × be, keep in bondage, be bondmen, bond-service, compel, do, dress, ear, execute, + husbandman, keep, labour (-ing man), bring to pass, (cause to, make to) serve (-ing, self), (be, become) servant (-s), do (use) service, till (-er), transgress [from margin], (set a) work, be wrought, **worshipper**.

Hand - a primitive word; a hand (**the open one [indicating power, means, direction, etc.**], in distinction from <H3709> (kaph), the closed one); used (as noun, adverb, etc.) in a great variety of applications, both literal and figurative, both proximate and remote [as follow] :- (+ be) able, × about, + armholes, at, axletree, because of, beside, border, × **bounty**, + broad, [broken-] handed, × by, charge, coast, + consecrate, + creditor, custody, debt, dominion, × enough, + fellowship, force, × from, hand [-staves, -y work], × he, himself, × in, labour, + large, ledge, [left-] handed, means, × mine, ministry, near, × of, × order, ordinance, × our, parts, pain, power, × presumptuously, service, side, sore, state, stay, draw with strength, stroke, + swear, terror, × thee, × by them, × themselves, × thine own, × thou, through, × throwing, + thumb, times, × to, × under, × us, × wait on, [way-] side, where, + wide, × with (him, me, you), work, + yield, × yourselves.

Man - from <H119> ("adam); ruddy, i.e. a human being (an individual or the species, mankind, etc.) :- × another, + hypocrite, + common sort, × low, man (mean, of low degree), person; to show blood (in the face), i.e. flush or turn rosy :- be (dyed, made) red (ruddy).

Knows - a primitive root; to know (properly to **ascertain by seeing**); used in a great variety of senses, figurative, literal, euphemism and inference (including observation, care, **recognition;** and causative **instruction**, designation, punishment, etc.) [as follow] :- acknowledge, acquaintance (-ted with), advise, answer, appoint, assuredly, be aware, [un-] awares, can [-not], certainly, for a certainty, **comprehend**, consider, × could they, cunning, declare, be diligent, (can, cause to) discern, discover, endued with, familiar friend, famous, feel, can have, be [ig-] norant, instruct, kinsfolk, kinsman, (cause to, let, make) know, (come to give, have, take) knowledge, have [knowledge], (be, make, make to be, make self) known, + **be learned**, + lie by man, mark, **perceive**, privy to, × prognosticator, regard, have respect, skilful, shew, can (man of) skill, be sure, of a surety, teach, (can) tell, understand, have [understanding], × will be, wist, wit, wot.

Love - feminine of <H158> ("ahab) and meaning the same :- love; from <H157> ("ahab); affection (in a good or a bad sense) :- love (-r); or "aheb, aw-habe"; a primitive root; to have affection for (sexually or otherwise) :- (be-) love (-d, -ly, -r), like, friend.

Hatred - from <H8130> (sane"); hate :- + exceedingly, hate (-ful, -red); a primitive root; to hate (personal) :- enemy, foe, (be) hate (-ful, -r), odious, × utterly.

CHAPTER 21

Einstein, A Missed Photo Op

Isaiah 43:18-19 (KJV)

18 Remember (mark so as to be recognized, remember, mention, recount or think on) ye not the former things (ancestors, of old time, your past; a beginning; to shake the head), neither consider (separate, distinguish, understand, have intelligence) the things of old (anterior, ancient, they that went before).

19 Behold, I will do a new thing (new, fresh; be new, rebuild, renew, repair); now it shall spring forth (sprout, bear, bring forth, bud, grow); shall ye not know (know by seeing, observe)it? I will even make (put, appoint, give, heap up, reward) a way (road, course, mode of action) in the wilderness (in the sense of driving, a pasture, a desert, in speech; to arrange words, answer, appoint, declare, promise, pronounce, utter), and rivers (a stream, prosperity, sparkle, be cheerful, to flow, be lightened) in the desert (desolation, desert, solitary; to lie waste).

These two sentences tell us to not look back. Don't look at what you did or accomplished or how you may have acted. Don't look back at what your parents, your grandparents or further back did or who they may have been in the social or economic charts. Looking back can be a trap no matter whether what you are looking back at was good or bad.

If what you saw happen to your family or your people was wonderful, you may look at this as “how am I ever going to measure up?” If what you see when you look is bad, it is easy to fall into the trap of self-pity or anger. You may consider that there was so much that has gone wrong that it is too late for things to go well for you now.

God wants us to look at each day as fresh and new. He is rebuilding, renewing and repairing anything that was broken. He wants us in the “now” because every new second is fresh with its own possibilities. We are to continue to look forward, and when we choose to do so there is a commitment of increase is in front of us.

Looking back can slow you down and worse yet, it can cause you to stumble and fall. If we continue to look backward we may miss these gifts, a new path, and even the right words to speak in a new situation.

He has prosperity, cheerfulness, light-heartedness for us even in the midst of what may appear on the surface a waste land. You may be facing a new phase in your life that appears to be a setback. Setbacks can be hard for us to deal with, but we don’t see things the way he does.

I was watching Einstein on the History channel a while back. This is my understanding from the documentary. When he went to college he was a lady’s man, he was a thinker, he wanted to understand from God how the things of the universe worked. Physics was his area of study. People didn’t think of him as a scientist; they weren’t sure he would succeed in school or after. When he graduated he couldn't get a job.

His father wrote letters and spoke to people so that he could become a teacher or professor, anything that was worthy. Instead, he got a job that a friend helped him get in the patent office as a 3rd grade patent clerk. His father died thinking he was a failure. These plans for inventions would come across his desk, he would do his patent "thing" and then had hours daily to look out the window of this upper floor office and ponder.

He wrote his first few papers from his time in the patent office. Then he took on the law of gravity (Sir Isaac Newton) and wrote his first paper on relativity. It was pretty far out there but, one eminent person in the field of physics thought this person might just be onto something.

Well the only way to prove out his theory was to have a series of pictures taken during a solar eclipse. These pictures had to be taken from two separate locations in Russia. Two men went to Russia for him. One was German, one American.

Just as they were in the two chosen locations, Germany declared war on Russia, and the project fell apart. No pictures and therefore no validation of the theory. He was once again delayed.

The story is long but he finally had secured a position in a prestigious university. His theory was not proven for many, many years. Before it was, during the review and more concentrated thought (if you can imagine more) he found that his mathematic calculation of this was incorrect.

Had those two photographers been able to take those pictures he would have been disgraced.

So although he was delayed it served the purpose of keeping him from public disgrace that may have kept him from presenting any of his future ideas or having them accepted by his peers and the world.

Here was a man that in his college years people would never label as a genius, in his early years after college was a clerk and certainly not recognized as a genius (often considered harebrained). He was married to his wife who was also a physic major in college.

They had two children, but their marriage was riddled with jealousy. His wife was jealous on two fronts. Although she was his sounding board for these theories and helped him type his papers and although the theories were not hers, his eventual recognition pushed them apart. Then when he was hired as a scientist at university he became emotionally attached to his cousin.

He and his wife, were separated by both physical miles and marital betrayal, were eventually divorced. The war came, and he was one of four professors in a college full of his peers who were against formulating the chlorine gas used to kill so many. Yet he persevered, instead of looking back, he continued to look forward. He faced people not believing in him, family issues, the problems of wars, having to keep secret some of his ideas so that others would not claim the recognition given for the discovery, and yet moved forward.

Good morning, Father. Thank you so much for a beautiful day, a fresh new day, a day to rebuild and restore what may have appeared to be lost. Thank you for new things energetically bursting into our lives and that we will know it when it comes. You give us ideas, means to get there, words to speak to others and over our lives. You are bringing us streams of prosperity in the desolate areas of our lives. As this begins to appear in our lives, we ask that you show us how to use best what you have provided, show us the people and organizations that we are to support, open our eyes and hearts to them. We praise and thank you for it in Jesus' name, Amen!

Definitions for today's study:

Remember - a primitive root; properly **to mark (so as to be recognized)**, i.e. to remember; by implication **to mention**; also (as denominative from <H2145> (zakar)) to be male :- × burn [incense], × earnestly, be male, (make) mention (of), be mindful, **recount**, record (-er), remember, make to be remembered, bring (call, come, keep, put) to (in) remembrance, × still, **think on**, × well.

Consider - a primitive root; **to separate mentally** (or **distinguish**), i.e. (general) **understand** :- attend, consider, be cunning, diligently, direct, discern, eloquent, feel, inform, instruct, **have intelligence**, know, look well to, mark, perceive, be prudent, regard, (can) skill (-ful), teach, think, (cause, make to, get, give, have) understand (-ing), view, (deal) wise (-ly, man).

Old - or qadmoniy, kad-mo-nee"; from <H6930> (qadmown); (of time) **anterior [earlier in time, near the front of a part of your body]** or (of place) oriental :- **ancient**, **they that went before**, east, (thing of) old; from <H6923> (qadam); *eastern* :- east; a primitive root; **to *project* (one self)**, i.e. ***precede [to happen or exist before]***; hence to *anticipate, hasten, meet* (usually for help) :- come (go, [flee]) before, + disappoint, meet, prevent.

CHAPTER 22

One Step Forward, Two Steps Back

Psalm 45:1 (KJV)

1 My heart (feelings, will, intellect, mental comfort, courage, understanding, wisdom) is indicting (to gush-flow quickly and in large quantities, unrestrained expression of emotion; praise enthusiastically; a sudden stream or jet; express admiration or pleasure with so much enthusiasm that people think you are not sincere) a good matter (a word, thing or cause; business; to arrange): I speak (admit openly, make no bones about it; discover by examining evidence, determine with certainty) of the things which I have made (an action, abstract activity, a product, business, occupation, thing offered, operation, possession, exercise, fashion, journey) touching the king (royal, to reign, ascend the throne, take counsel, rule): my tongue (instrument to lick, eat, speak; speech, an ingot-a block of gold, silver, or other metal shaped for convenient handling) is the pen of a ready (quick, skillful, diligent) writer (to score with a mark as a tally or record, inscribe, innumerate, recount, celebrate, shew forth, tell, talk).

This verse combines the power three; thought, speech, and action. It tells of how these things used in unison begin to paint the picture of a good future. There are some areas that God's principles require our participation, this is one of them. Whether you realize it or not you already engage in the power three. You have created your present and are creating your future, too.

This is a verse that records the physical/material enactment by us on earth of the instruction of the spiritual power three; God the Father, Jesus the Son and the Holy Spirit our Counselor.

Today we will look at this in Genesis 1:26 (KJV) And God said, Let us make man in our image, after our likeness: and let them have dominion over the fish of the sea, and over the fowl of the air, and over the cattle, and over all the earth, and over every creeping thing that creepeth upon the earth.

He also states that "His thoughts are higher than our thoughts." So the thought process was born of God. As is the speech and action part of our being. God created the earth and His Spirit moved upon the face of the waters. And when God said, creation happened.

Once the spoken word is out there in the atmosphere, action begins on both a spiritual and physical sides of the coin. Spiritually our speech brings forces into play we don't see. Physically we move on the things we give voice to.

That is why it is so important to first harness the thought process. Then we can dwell on the thoughts in our mind that are based on God principles and discard all others. The reason is that what we dwell on, we end up speaking about. And what we speak about we act on.

Not only do we act on these thoughts, but whatever we think, speak and act on is drawn into us. Our words act as a magnetic force pulling people, circumstances and even things into our lives.

We frequently see that we take one step forward and two steps back. You might ask why this happens. Depending on how strong wrong thoughts have been imbedded in our minds; it may take a while longer for some than others to be consistent in the discipline of thought and speech.

From my own experience, I can attest to the fact that changing unproductive mindsets into solely productive ones is a process and normally doesn't happen in one fell swoop. It would be great if it did, but we are cautioned throughout the text to guard our hearts and minds because ungodly thoughts continue to attempt to get past our mind gate. Happily, we get better and better at thinking right things and discarding wrong thought.

It is a bit of a dance, however, the more consistent we become in entertaining Godly thought, the more good and prosperous increase we will see played out in our lives.

This verse speaks of "gushing" an unrestrained expression of good matters. And when we do express ourselves in this manner, we touch the king. Who would have thought our words mean so much to God?

Good morning, Father. Thank you so much for showing us the necessity of the power three. We can only do in the physical realm what you have given us to do with the help of our spiritual power three. We open ourselves today to your direction, your means and your resources. We open ourselves to grace for help with our shortcomings and favor that supersedes our need. We give you our lives to serve those we have been assigned to. You have shown us our life is not segmented into family, business, and spiritual, instead our lives have all aspects melded together. Spirit is a part of all we do. There is no separation of material and spiritual, but that every material thing has a base of spirit, you show us this in your creation of us and this earth. Life above all is spiritual and played out in a physical realm. Thank you for every person who reads this prayer, for their place and occupation, and for helping us to identify where we can best serve. In Jesus' holy name, we praise and thank you, Amen!

Definitions used in today's study:

Inditing - a primitive root; to gush :- indite.

Speak - a primitive root; to say (used with great latitude) :- answer, appoint, avouch, bid, boast self, call, certify, challenge, charge, + (at the, give) command (-ment), commune, consider, declare, demand, × desire, determine, × expressly, × indeed, × intend, name, × plainly, promise, publish, report, require, say, speak (against, of), × still, × suppose, talk, tell, term, × that is, × think, use [speech], utter, × verily, × yet.

Made - from <H6213> (\`asah); an action (good or bad); generally a transaction; abstract activity; by implication a product (specifically a poem) or (generic) property :- act, art, + bakemeat, business, deed, do (-ing), labour, thing made, ware of making, occupation, thing offered, operation, possession, × well, ([handy-, needle-, net-]) work, (-ing, -manship), wrought.

Tongue - or lashon, law-shone'; also (in plural) feminine leshonah, lesh-o-naw'; from <H3960> (lashan); the tongue (of man or animals), used literal (as the instrument of licking, eating, or speech), and figurative (speech, an ingot, a fork of flame, a cove of water) :- + babbler, bay, + evil speaker, language, talker, tongue, wedge.

CONCLUSION

You may choose to get the wisdom of God's process of thought a little deeper in you understanding. To do this daily confession is one of the best tools I know. I have personalized these so that you can speak these as yours, if not you can just go to your Bible and speak the words as they are written aloud. Verses include Strong's Concordance and dictionary definitions in parentheses and underlined.

This is how this would look as my daily confession:

Colossians 3:2 (KJV)

I set my affection (exercise my mind, entertain or have sentiment or opinion, am mentally disposed or make receptive or involve my mind or intellectual process/willing towards an action or attitude or belief) on things above, not on things on the earth.

Matthew 16:23 (KJV)

, Get thee behind me, Satan: thou art an offence unto me: for thou savourest (exercise the mind toward, entertain, be disposed to, interest oneself in) not the things that be of God, but those that be of men.

Mark 8:33 (KJV)

, Get thee behind me, Satan: for thou savourest (exercise the mind toward, entertain, be disposed to, interest oneself in) not the things that be of God, but the things that be of men.

Acts 28:22 (KJV)

But we desire (deem entitled or fit) to hear of thee what thou thinkest (exercise the mind, have an opinion): for as concerning this sect (a party, disunion), we know that every where it is spoken against.

Romans 12:2 (KJV)

I am not (qualified negation) conformed (to fashion alike, make in an image like, in its pattern) to this world (an age, course): but am transformed (have a completely different form or appearance) by the **renewing** (renovation, act of restoring to its former good condition) of my mind (the intellect: creative use of mind, ability to understand complicated subjects), that I may prove what is that good, and acceptable, and perfect, will of God. (for me)

Joshua 1:8 (KJV)

This book of the Word will not depart out of my mouth (skirt); but I will meditate in it day and night, that I may observe to do according to all that is written therein: for then I shalt make thy way prosperous, and then I will have good success.

Proverbs 23:6 (KJV)

I eat (feed on, set all your attention on, interest) not the bread (food) of him that hath an evil eye (discernment, clever idea, subject), neither do I desire (have in mind) his dainty meats (to perceive):

Proverbs 23:7 (KJV)

For as I think (to split open, act as gate-keeper, estimate, use or exercise the mind) in my heart, so am I,

Romans 12:3 (KJV)

For I say, through the grace given unto me, I don't think of myself more highly than I ought to think; but I think (exercise the mind) soberly (be of sound mind, in right mind, self-controlled, temperate or not given to extreme behavior or language), according (in that manner, in agreement with, because of the reason given) as God (the supreme Divinity, magistrate) hath dealt (distribute, divide, a division or share) to me the measure (expressing a particular quantity) of faith (persuasion, moral conviction, reliance upon Christ, have confidence, increasingly confident).

Philippians 3:13 (KJV)

I count not myself to have apprehended: but this one thing I do, forgetting (neglect, lie hidden, be ignorant, unawares) those things which are behind, and reaching forth unto (stretching, extend to) those things which are before (in front of),

Hebrews 6:12 (KJV)

I am not slothful (sluggish, lazy, stupid, dull), but a follower of them who through faith (persuasion, moral conviction, be or increase in confidence) and patience (good-natured tolerance, ability to be polite, calm and patient in hard times, strength of mind enabling to endure) inherit the promises.

1 Peter 5:8 (KJV)

I am sober (discreet, abstain from wine, watch, approach with a serious attitude), and vigilant (to keep awake, idea of collecting one's faculties, rouse from sleep); because my adversary (an opponent, the opposite of right and justice) the devil (a traducer, false accuser, slanderer), as a roaring lion, walks about, seeking whom he may devour (to drink down, swallow up): and he may not devour me.

Ephesians 4:23 (KJV)

I am renewed (renovated, reformed – change that is intended to correct a situation) in the spirit (mental disposition – a tendency to behave in a certain way, the Spirit of God) of your mind (the intellect, understanding, be sure);

Ecclesiastes 9:1 (KJV)

For all this I considered (admit openly, make no bones about it; discover by examining evidence, determine with certainty) in my heart (feelings, will, intellect, understanding, wisdom) even to declare all this, that the righteous, and the wise, and their works, are in the hand of God: no man knows either love or hatred by all that is before them.

Isaiah 43:18-19 (KJV)

I remember (mark so as to be recognized, remember, mention, recount or think on) not the former things (ancestors, of old time, your past; a beginning; to shake the head), neither do I consider (separate, distinguish, understand, have intelligence) the things of old (anterior, ancient, they that went before).

Behold, You are doing a new thing (new, fresh; be new, rebuild, renew, repair); now it shall spring forth (sprout, bear, bring forth, bud, grow); will I not know it (know by seeing, observe)it? You have made (put, appoint, give, heap up, reward) a way (road, course, mode of action) in the wilderness (in the sense of driving, a pasture, a desert, in speech; to arrange words, answer, appoint, declare, promise, pronounce, utter), and rivers (a stream, prosperity, sparkle, be cheerful, to flow, be lightened) in the desert (desolation, desert, solitary; to lie waste) for me.

Psalm 45:1 (KJV)

My heart (feelings, will, intellect, mental comfort, courage, understanding, wisdom) is indicting (to gush - flow quickly and in large quantities, unrestrained expression of emotion; praise enthusiastically; a sudden stream or jet; express admiration or pleasure with so much enthusiasm that people think you are not sincere) a good matter (a word, thing or cause; business; to arrange): I speak (admit openly, make no bones about it; discover by examining evidence, determine with certainty) of the things which I have made (an action, abstract activity, a product, business, occupation, thing offered, operation, possession, exercise, fashion, journey) touching the king (royal, to reign, ascend the throne, take counsel, rule): my tongue (instrument to lick, eat, speak; speech, an ingot - a block of gold, silver, or other metal shaped for convenient handling) is the pen of a ready (quick, skillful, diligent) writer (to score with a mark as a tally or record, inscribe, innumerate, recount, celebrate, show forth, tell, talk).

Tarshish Productions

1933 N Stone Maple Ln

Elkhart, Indiana 47514

www.lindacnewberry.com

info@lindacnewberry.com

www.ingramcontent.com/pod-product-compliance
Lightning Source LLC
LaVergne TN
LVHW020636100826
845148LV00012B/2197

* 9 7 8 0 9 7 6 9 6 4 0 6 3 *